Marvelous Faith

Marvelous Faith

Showing a Level of Belief That Amazes God

Raymond K. Shin
Foreword by John Carroll Byrnes

RESOURCE *Publications* · Eugene, Oregon

MARVELOUS FAITH
Showing a Level of Belief That Amazes God

Copyright © 2022 Raymond K. Shin. All rights reserved. Except for brief quotations in critical publications or reviews, no part of this book may be reproduced in any manner without prior written permission from the publisher. Write: Permissions, Wipf and Stock Publishers, 199 W. 8th Ave., Suite 3, Eugene, OR 97401.

Resource Publications
An Imprint of Wipf and Stock Publishers
199 W. 8th Ave., Suite 3
Eugene, OR 97401

www.wipfandstock.com

PAPERBACK ISBN: 978-1-6667-3436-2
HARDCOVER ISBN: 978-1-6667-9013-9
EBOOK ISBN: 978-1-6667-9014-6

July 22, 2022 10:32 AM

Unless otherwise indicated, all Scripture quotations are from the *ESV® Bible (The Holy Bible, English Standard Version®)*, copyright © 2001 by Crossway, a publishing ministry of Good News Publishers. Used by permission. All rights reserved.

In regard to Scripture quotations from The Authorized (King James) Version: Rights in the Authorized Version in the United Kingdom are vested in the Crown. Reproduced by permission of the Crown's patentee, Cambridge University Press.

Scripture quotations from the New International Version are taken from the Holy Bible, New International Version®, NIV®. Copyright © 1973, 1978, 1984, 2011 by Biblica, Inc.™ Used by permission of Zondervan. All rights reserved worldwide. www.zondervan.com. The "NIV" and "New International Version" are trademarks registered in the United States Patent and Trademark Office by Biblica, Inc.™

To Yusun, Julia & Emily.

Contents

Foreword by John Carroll Byrnes | ix

Preface | xiii

Acknowledgments | xv

Introduction | xix

1. What Is Faith? | 1
2. How Do We Obtain Faith? | 7
3. How Do We Maintain Faith? | 22
4. Where Does Faith Lead? | 47

Conclusion | 63

Bibliography | 67

Foreword

IN 2014, THE *NEW YORK TIMES* published a column that presented a spiritual statistical reality check: 28 percent believed the Bible is the "actual word of God," 47 percent believed it is the "inspired word of God," and 21 percent believed the Bible is an "ancient book of fables, legends, history, and moral precepts."[1] Fast forward to a more recent report:

> In recent years, the share of American adults who do not affiliate with a religious group has risen dramatically. In spite of this trend, the overwhelming majority of Americans, including a majority of the religiously unaffiliated—those who describe themselves, religiously, as atheists, agnostics or "nothing in particular"—say they believe in God or a higher power, according to a new Pew Research Center survey conducted in December of 2017. At the same time, only a slim majority of Americans now believe in the God of the Bible and roughly one-in-ten U.S. adults don't believe in any higher power or spiritual force.[2]

And faster forward to 2022 and it is plain to see that affiliation with organized religion has declined, perhaps because of some scandals or possibly COVID-induced spiritual lethargy.

One of the other reasons for the apparent relative decline in public appreciation of organized religion may be that the biblical

---

1. Blow, "Religious Constriction."
2. Fahmy, "Key Findings."

teaching and literature is, in a word, "dated," meaning that the vocabulary, historical references, and context are not readily understood by many twenty-first century readers. Think of the average high school student enjoying social media, sparse journalism, and typical video entertainment. This is a motive for the nascent "J Book Project" with which Ray Shin and I are also associated—to translate Jesus' important sayings into easily accessible English and thereby compliment the many scholarly and contemporary texts, including the rich literature of weekly church-based sermons.

This title is a kindred spirit. Ray Shin beautifully captures the substance and spirit of the Christian canon and presents it to contemporary readers lucidly and artfully. After all, isn't that the point? Jesus came to save and redeem by teaching invaluable moral lessons, and who would deny that such lessons, moral advisories if you will, are of inestimable intellectual and spiritual value today? Contemporary media and entertainment are implicitly dishing out such moral standards, some to the public good and some not so much, 24/7. As a consequence, it is well understood by students of human nature that many beliefs, mundane and sublime, are often susceptible to a variety of influences often leading to what might be called the waxing and waning syndrome.

In chapter 3, Ray Shin includes this memorable text with a quotation from C. S. Lewis: "As the fictional high-ranking demon Screwtape observes, all humans are prone to the 'law of Undulation,' which is 'the repeated return to a level from which [people] repeatedly fall back, a series of troughs and peaks.' And undulation affects everything we do, not just faith in God." It is probably incontestable that Christian messages and endeavors benefit from dialogue inside and out of the boundaries of traditional Christian gatherings, even given the human reality that such dialogues can deteriorate into uncharitable rancor. We remember that early Christians often discussed the message of Jesus by imagery along with spoken word, and those artful messages enhanced those teachings. Now we benefit from orated, written, and artful presentations of what Jesus said.

Foreword

But that Christian symphony of text, art, and speech did not eliminate the potential for disagreement. Think of the life of Episcopal Bishop John Shelby Spong, who died in 2021. He was both a persuasive intellectual pioneer and a spiritual provocateur. He challenged Christians today to think about this essential question: "What's it all about?" Regardless of your thoughts on Bishop Spong's theology, we all benefit from thoughtful and contemporary presentations of the Word, perhaps particularly those emanating from the author's young generation.

John Carroll Byrnes
Baltimore

Preface

I'm not going through "a mid-life crisis" (at least I don't think I am), but when I turned forty years old, I realized that I'm about halfway toward the end of my statistical life expectancy.[1] Yes, I know that's a bit morbid, but this realization has made me take stock of how I've ended up where I am in life. I've also begun thinking more about where I'm headed and what I may leave behind. The big four-oh has made me assess myself, which I believe is a good thing.

One very important aspect of my life is my faith. But until now, I've never really examined why faith is so important to me. What am I believing? And am I exhibiting a faith that positively affects others around me? This book is an attempt to help me answer those questions, so I've written it in some way for myself. Writing something that others might read forces me to organize my thoughts and beliefs, which in turn helps me check myself.

But I don't want this to be just about me. I also hope this book is an encouragement to others to see why it's worth pursuing faith even when it gets really difficult. It's a part of the human condition to go through really challenging seasons in life, and sometimes those painful periods are so intense that it can make you question the point of it all. Anybody can feel that way. Even Rev. Lovejoy in an episode of *The Simpsons* doubts his faith when it seems that the

---

1. The average forty-year-old male in the United States in 2018 was expected to live until he reaches 80.8 years old. Arias and Xu, "United States Life Tables, 2018."

Preface

leader of the Movementarians cult is actually going to fly to Blisstonia in his spaceship.[2] Humorous cartoons aside, people in high positions of faith can be shaken too during the trials of life. However, I believe that faith becomes stronger by striving to maintain it with God's help through difficult periods, and this is possible for everybody. Not only that, the Bible shows that we can even get to a point where God marvels at our faith.

Before we continue, I'd like to acknowledge that I'm not a biblical scholar or a member of the clergy. I'm a lay member of a church trying to live life the right way—being a good husband, father, son, employee, friend, and citizen. And I'm trying to live right through a proper understanding and exercise of faith. I fail much too often at doing that, but I want to keep trying. This book is an attempt to remind myself why I need to keep at it, and I hope you find encouragement in it too.

Any shortcomings you discover in my analysis of the Bible are certainly unintended. Although I'm not without expertise in theology and biblical analysis, I acknowledge that I'm not a professional in those fields. But I trust that such shortcomings don't detract from what I ultimately wish to share: as hard as it might be, it is very possible to possess and exhibit a faith that makes God be taken aback in amazement. And that faith can lead us truly to love others, especially those who really need love.

Ray Shin
February 28, 2022
Gaithersburg, Maryland

---

2. Moore, "Joy of Sect." During the climax of that episode, Rev. Lovejoy nervously exclaims, "Oh mercy! He's the real deal!" and stomps on his clerical collar after tearing it off and throwing it on the ground.

Acknowledgments

I'd like to thank some special people who took the time to help with this book and provide insightful recommendations to improve it:

- The Hon. John C. Byrnes. A dear person in my life to whom I was assigned almost twenty years ago in a law school mentor program. When we first met, he warned he may not have much to impart to me because he was a *retired* judge. (Yes, I remember him emphasizing "retired.") He vastly undersold himself. Judge Byrnes continues to be a mentor to me not just in my practice of law, but also much more importantly in my general life. He has read through multiple drafts of this book, and he helped me economize the language in it and present my ideas more crisply.

- Janet Kim. My cousin helped make sure that what's written here makes sense and corrected many wayward citations, some of which were plain embarrassing on my part. I thank her for patiently combing through this thing when it was a mess and withholding judgment where I fall short.

- Julie Kim. A friend who helped me keep focus on what exactly I want to share and encouraged me to keep digging deeper into the messages behind the Bible stories that are recounted in this book. And she encouraged me to try finding a publisher for this book despite my doubts about such an endeavor.

Acknowledgments

- Kathleen King. My colleague at work without whom our office would fall apart. I've always appreciated our conversations about not only work but about life, and she talked to me about this book with the expansive view of life that she so brightly displays at work every day. My conversations with her reminded me to keep this book "real" in a way that can hopefully be an encouragement to readers in their day-to-day lives.

- Justin Kuruvilla. A cherished friend since that day in sixth grade when we sat together by chance on the school bus. His family has treated me not only to many delicious meals over the decades but also to the rich tradition of the Syrian Orthodox Church, which has shaped my deeper reverence for Saint Thomas the Apostle, whom I discuss in chapter 3.

- Aaron Shin. My brother who has a knack for connecting with people. He reviewed this book and encouraged me to find more and better ways to connect with readers through relatable stories and illustrations.

Additionally, I'm thankful to my Bible study group at Open Door Presbyterian Church in Herndon, Virginia. When we meet on Friday evenings, we read through Bible passages and talk through how they apply to us and our families, neighborhoods, and workplaces. Our countless discussions through the years have led me to ponder and wrestle with many points that I touch in this book. I'm grateful to our group leader, Mic Garcia, who has always been very well prepared to guide our lively talks that often run deep into the night, and to my fellow Bible study group members who are never too shy to share their rich insights: Mic's wife Susan Garcia; Tae and Michelle Lee-Kwon; Ellen Park; and my wife, Yusun Lee.

Finally, I'd like to thank all of my coworkers in the office. We work in a corner of the federal government that could easily feel overwhelming if we let it. The potential exists for immense stress and burnout as we pursue our agency's mission of helping people before, during, and after disasters. I'm also aware that it could be

Acknowledgments

even worse for people like me working in the legal department; it's my observation that attorneys by nature tend to be susceptible to overworking themselves. Yet, I'm very lucky to work in a federal agency and a legal office that truly wants the employees to take care of themselves and each other, which has allowed me to find enough time and strength to pursue personal interests like working on this book.

Introduction

IS IT POSSIBLE FOR God to marvel at anything we do? It makes sense for the reverse to be true: that humans would marvel at the works of an omnipotent and omniscient God. But as difficult as it might be to believe, the Bible recounts a time when Jesus is astonished by a mortal man.[1] What made Jesus so amazed was the man's faith.

A Roman centurion's servant is sick and about to die.[2] When the centurion hears that Jesus is in town, he sends some people to ask him to heal his servant.[3] Jesus obliges and begins making his

---

1. This account appears twice in the Bible: Matt 8:5–13 and Luke 7:1–10. There are differences between those accounts, and one explanation for some of the differences is that Matthew's gospel was written for the Jewish audience and emphasized the centurion's faith, and Luke's gospel was intended for the Gentiles (i.e., non-Jewish people) and focused on the good relationship between the Roman centurion and Jewish teachers. *Life Application Study Bible*, 1738. I draw from both accounts to retell this story of the centurion.

2. The centurion is in Jesus' part of the world because Rome conquered Israel in 64 BC. See, e.g., Puskas and Robbins, *Introduction to the New Testament*, 33. It's interesting to note that while there are many stories of people asking Jesus to heal their family and friends, this is the only time in the Bible when someone asks Jesus to heal a servant. Henry, *Commentary on the Whole Bible*, 1648.

3. The account in Matthew states that the centurion himself went to Jesus, but the seeming discrepancy may be explained like this: "[I]t is a rule that *we are said to do that which we do by another—Quod facimus per alium, id ipsum facere judicamur*. The centurion might be said to do that which he did by his proxies; as a man takes possession by his attorney." Henry, *Commentary on the Whole Bible*, 1844 (emphasis in original). See also *ESV Study Bible*, 1835 ("[Matthew] actually reports what the centurion said *through* his messengers,

xix

INTRODUCTION

way to the centurion's house, but the centurion sends others to tell Jesus: "Lord, do not trouble yourself, for I am not worthy to have you come under my roof. Therefore I did not presume to come to you. But say the word, and let my servant be healed. For I too am a man set under authority, with soldiers under me: and I say to one, 'Go,' and he goes; and to another, 'Come,' and he comes; and to my servant, 'Do this,' and he does it."[4] Hearing this, Jesus is said to "marvel" at the centurion, and he exclaims that he has never seen such great faith. Another translation of the Bible that is written in more contemporary English captures his utter astonishment by saying that Jesus is "taken aback" by the centurion's display of faith.[5] The account ends with Jesus saying to the centurion: "Go; let it be done for you as you have believed," and the servant is healed "at that very moment."

In the original Greek,[6] Matthew and Luke use the word *thaumazó* to describe Jesus' reaction to the centurion's faith, which can be translated as "to wonder" and, by implication, "admire" and "marvel."[7] It is the same Greek word used many times elsewhere in the New Testament to describe people marveling at the miracles of Jesus (even if the word has been translated into different words

based on the idea that what a person does through an agent is what the person himself does" [Emphasis in original]).

4. Luke 7:6–8.

5. Peterson, *Message* (describing Jesus as being "taken aback" in both Matt 8:10 and Luke 7:9).

6. Even though Aramaic was the native tongue of Jesus and many of his contemporaries, the New Testament was originally written in vernacular Greek, which had become the *lingua franca* across the Mediterranean world as a result of Alexander the Great's conquests 300 years earlier. Puskas and Robbins, *Introduction to the New Testament*, 3–5. Even after the Roman Empire's subsequent conquests of those same lands, Latin did not replace common Greek as the universal language across the Mediterranean world until the fourth century. McCarthy, "Challenge of Translation," 133. See also Macfarlane, "Hebrew, Aramaic, Greek, and Latin."

7. Strong, *New Exhaustive Concordance*, s.v. "θαυμάζω" (Greek entry no. 2296). I'm going to throw around Greek words at the risk of seeming more learned than I really am, but I don't know a lick of Greek. I just think that it helps to be mindful of the original language in which a book is written. It provides important context to what the work is trying to convey.

INTRODUCTION

in English), like when he calms a furious storm after rebuking it[8] and performs a number of miraculous healings in a single session.[9] It's also the same word used to report how people react when he argues with religious experts on whether to pay taxes to Caesar[10] and when he breaks rigid cultural norms by conversing with a Samaritan woman.[11] Additionally, this word describes how people witness the miracles that the apostles later perform in Jesus' name,[12] and the word is used to convey how Moses reacted upon seeing the burning bush.[13]

---

8. Matt 8:27 ("And the men marveled, saying, 'What sort of man is this, that even winds and sea obey him?'"); Mark 6:51 ("And he got into the boat with them, and the wind ceased. And they were utterly astounded."); and Luke 8:25 ("He said to them, 'Where is your faith?' And they were afraid, and they marveled, saying to one another, 'Who then is this, that he commands even winds and water, and they obey him?'").

9. Matt 15:30–31 ("And great crowds came to him, bringing with them the lame, the blind, the crippled, the mute, and many others, and they put them at his feet, and he healed them, so that the crowd wondered, when they saw the mute speaking, the crippled healthy, the lame walking, and the blind seeing. And they glorified the God of Israel.").

10. Matt 22:21–22 ("Then [Jesus] said to them, 'Therefore render to Caesar the things that are Caesar's, and to God the things that are God's.' When [the Pharisees] heard it, they marveled. And they left him and went away."); Mark 12:17 ("Jesus said to them, 'Render to Caesar the things that are Caesar's, and to God the things that are God's.' And they marveled at him."); and Luke 20:26 ("And they were not able in the presence of the people to catch him in what he said, but marveling at his answer they became silent.").

11. John 4:27 ("Just then his disciples came back. They marveled that he was talking with a woman."). And this wasn't just any woman; she was a *Samaritan* woman. See John 4:9 ("The Samaritan woman said to him, 'How is it that you, a Jew, ask for a drink from me, a woman of Samaria?' [For Jews have no dealings with Samaritans.]").

12. See, e.g., Acts 3:12 (after healing a crippled beggar, Peter asks the astonished crowd: "Men of Israel, why do you wonder at this, or why do you stare at us, as though by our own power or piety we have made him walk?"). The King James Version might be a better translation of the Greek word *thaumazó* in that verse: "And when Peter saw it, he answered unto the people, Ye men of Israel, why marvel ye at this?"

13. Acts 7:31 (quoting Stephen: "When Moses saw [the burning bush], he was amazed at the sight").

Introduction

Here's what I find so interesting about this story of the centurion: the use of the word *thaumazó* indicates to me that Jesus was astonished in a similar way (if not the same way) as people who were amazed at his miracles or how Moses was amazed to discover the burning bush.[14] If Jesus is God as Christians believe,[15] and if God is omniscient,[16] how could Jesus be surprised or taken aback by anything? I don't know how to reconcile the paradox of an all-knowing God being amazed and astonished at the action of a created human being, and I'm not going to try because this is way beyond my inadequate intelligence and training. But I can say this: there is something powerful and otherworldly about the kind of amazing faith that the centurion exhibited to make Jesus marvel.

As an aside, it's interesting to note one other time when the Greek word *thaumazó* describes people doing something to make Jesus marvel. It was when people exhibited a *lack* of faith. Jesus goes to his hometown of Nazareth and teaches in the synagogue, but the congregants "took offense at him" because they wonder how Mary's son—who is a humble carpenter—can impart such wisdom.[17] The Bible then says, "And [Jesus] marveled because of

---

14. I'm using the words "marvel," "amaze," and "astonish" (along with their derivatives) interchangeably based on the definition of "marvel" as "to become filled with surprise, wonder, or *amazed* curiosity" and as "to feel *astonishment* or perplexity at or about" (Merriam-Webster, "marvel," https://www.merriam-webster.com/dictionary/marvel [emphases added]).

15. See, e.g., Matt 1:23 ("'Behold, the virgin shall conceive and bear a son, and they shall call his name Immanuel' [which means, God with us])"; John 8:58 (Jesus referring to himself as "I am," which is what God told Moses to call him in Exod 3:13–14); John 20:28 (after doubting, Thomas exclaims to Jesus, "My Lord and my God!"); and Col 2:9 ("For in him the whole fullness of deity dwells bodily"). See also Lewis, *Mere Christianity*, 51–52 (arguing that Jesus either is God or was a "lunatic" when he claimed to forgive any and all sins); Boyd and Boyd, *Letters from a Skeptic*; and Strobel, *Case for Christ*.

16. See, e.g., 1 Chr 28:9 (" . . . for the Lord searches all hearts and understands every plan and thought."); Jer 23:24 ("'Can a man hide himself in secret places so that I cannot see him?' declares the Lord. 'Do I not fill heaven and earth?' declares the Lord."); and 1 John 3:20 ("God is greater than our heart, and he knows everything.").

17. Matt 13:53–58; Mark 6:1–3.

INTRODUCTION

their unbelief."[18] But let's not talk about this any further; it's probably not a good thing to amaze God through a deficiency of faith. I think it's better to talk about the kind of faith that the centurion showed to amaze God.

So what is it about the centurion's faith that led God to marvel? And how can we be like that centurion? I believe that the centurion's variety of faith is characterized not so much by a certainty that God is all powerful and can do anything, although such certainty is important. Rather, the root of a faith that makes God marvel lies in a sure belief that we are made for God. It is an understanding that our meaning in life is based on being God's precious creation, which makes us want to maintain this faith so we can build a closer relationship with our loving Creator. This in turn leads to helping others realize this meaning in their lives.

The centurion's faith that astonished Jesus was a deep one that filled the core of his being, and I bet he ended up with this deeply burning faith only after cultivating it through difficult periods that sowed doubt. But after his faith withstood those tests, it became a part of him so that he used it to help others. In this case, the centurion's faith helped his servant experience the love and power of Jesus through healing from an ailment that threatened death.

There is thus a certain progression in faith, and I'd like to share my take on the centurion's kind of faith by following that progression. In chapter 1, I look into what faith is exactly. I then explore in chapters 2 and 3 how someone might obtain this deep faith and then maintain it. In chapter 4, I look into how obtaining and maintaining this faith causes us to look beyond ourselves and to share the faith with others through joy, hope, and love, which includes wanting to help the less fortunate be treated fairly and with care. In the end, I hope to show you and remind myself that anybody can possess an amazing faith that makes God marvel and brightens the lives of people around us.

---

18. Mark 6:6.

1

What Is Faith?

L ET'S SET THE STAGE by addressing the elementary question: What is faith? The Epistle to the Hebrews defines it like this: "Now faith is the assurance of things hoped for, the conviction of things not seen."[1] It's a deceptively simple definition, but it's packed with meaning.

Proof of Things Unseen

What is translated as "assurance" from the original Greek is the word "*hupostasis*." It means "a setting under (support)," which can be figurative language for "confidence" and "substance."[2] The essence of this word can be further understood from its use in the legal discourse of the day, in which the term meant a title deed or guarantee.[3] The writer of Hebrews is thus saying that faith is placing a support or guarantee under what we hope for. In other words, faith allows us to stand firm on solid ground believing that we will attain whatever we are hoping for.

---

1. Heb 11:1.
2. Strong, *New Exhaustive Concordance*, s.v. "ὑπόστασις" (Greek entry no. 5287).
3. Thompson, *Hebrews*, 230.

The verse doesn't stop at just saying that faith is having assurance of what we hope for. It continues by saying that faith is "the conviction of things not seen." The word "conviction" is used in a way that's not too common anymore. Here, the term can be defined in this instance as "the state of being convinced,"[4] which is in line with the original Greek *elegchos*, meaning "proof, conviction."[5] Perhaps the King James Version captures more from the original Greek, with emphasis added: "Now faith is the substance of things hoped for, the *evidence* of things not seen." Faith is thus the evidence, or proof, that convinces one of things that are unseen.

It's interesting that this verse speaks of faith in terms of what is not seen. We hope for a lot of things in life that our eyes can't necessarily see: intangible things like good health, security, proper education, recognition, admiration, and of course love. I'm not going to say that we need to deny ourselves those things. However, I think that the definition of faith in Heb 11:1 aims at far higher and weightier matters than even these very important intangible things. The faith described here reaches beyond the finite bounds of this world.

Eternity in Our Hearts

The author of Ecclesiastes observes that "[God] has put eternity into man's heart."[6] What does that mean? I'm picturing a heart with a bottomless hole that can never be filled fully by the things of the world. No matter how much money, love, achievements, and possessions you pour into that bottomless hole, it can never be filled, and we can never be satisfied. God has set eternity in our hearts, and no finite thing from this world can fill it. Only eternity can fill eternity, and only something (or someone) eternal can fill that bottomless hole in our hearts.

---

4. Merriam-Webster, "Conviction."

5. Strong, *New Exhaustive Concordance*, s.v. "ἔλεγχος" (Greek entry no. 1650). I apologize if all this Greek is Greek to you. I promise not to dig up any new Greek words.

6. Eccl 3:11.

What Is Faith?

Likewise, humans have been created in God's image and likeness.[7] This doesn't necessarily mean that we look physically like God, although I suppose we can't rule that out. God's image on humans is shown through our ability to exercise knowledge and pure goodness.[8] Does this not mean that we are most fully ourselves and meet our fullest potential when we decide to be with the good God who made us in his image and likeness?

This is why no matter how much we own in this world, we want more and more and end up being dissatisfied. The author of Ecclesiastes possessed more than anybody could ask for: houses; vineyards; gardens; parks; male and female slaves plus other slaves who were born in his house; more herds and flocks than anybody else had; silver and gold "and the treasure of kings and provinces"; men and women singers; and "many concubines."[9] But in the end, he laments, "He who loves money will not be satisfied with money, nor he who loves wealth with his income; this also is vanity."[10]

By "vanity," the author of Ecclesiastes isn't talking about anything related to conceit or pride. He's talking more in terms of how vain it was to accumulate all those treasures and other possessions. In the original Hebrew, the word used in that verse for "vanity" is one meaning "emptiness," or figuratively something transitory and unsatisfactory.[11] Those great but temporal things of the world, no matter how enticing and enjoyable, can't take the place of God in our hearts. The New International Version of the Bible captures the sentiment of the verse by translating the Hebrew term to say that it's all "meaningless."[12]

---

7. See, e.g., Gen 1:26–27 ("Then God said, 'Let us make man in our image, after our likeness.' . . . So God created man in his own image, in the image of God he created him; male and female he created them."); and Jas 3:9–10 ("With [the tongue] we bless our Lord and Father, and with it we curse people who are made in the likeness of God. From the same mouth come blessing and cursing. My brother, these things ought not to be so.").

8. Henry, *Commentary on the Whole Bible*, 6 (commenting on Gen 1:26).

9. Eccl 2:4–9.

10. Eccl 5:10.

11. Strong, *New Exhaustive Concordance*, s.v. "לָבָה" (Hebrew entry no. 1892).

12. Eccl. 5:10 in the New International Version is as follows: "Whoever

Is this not why so many of the rich and powerful appear on the news with divorces, financial ruin, and even suicide? I believe their plight is not different from less wealthy and famous people: no matter how much you amass, it's not enough to make you happy. And perhaps it's worse for those who have acquired so much. They know from personal experience that their great treasures and achievements don't satisfy whatever is eternally longing in their hearts. And when you consume everything you can possibly buy or otherwise acquire, what's left?

Filling the Eternity in Our Hearts

There is good news despite these perhaps melancholy observations. The fact that such an eternal longing in the heart exists is also evidence in and of itself that something can fill it. C. S. Lewis described the situation like this:

> Creatures are not born with desires unless satisfaction for those desires exists. A baby feels hunger: well, there is such a thing as food. A duckling wants to swim: well, there is such a thing as water. Men feel sexual desire: well, there is such a thing as sex. If I find in myself a desire which no experience in this world can satisfy, the most probable explanation is that I was made for another world. If none of my earthly pleasures satisfy it, that does not prove that the universe is a fraud. Probably earthly pleasures were never meant to satisfy it, but only arouse it, to suggest the real thing.[13]

As I heard a preacher describe it during a church retreat, all these things in the world that promise fulfillment are echoes of what God eternally provides for us.[14] He observed that the good

---

loves money never has enough; whoever loves wealth is never satisfied with their income. This too is meaningless."

13. Lewis, *Mere Christianity*, 136–37.

14. I sadly don't remember the name of the preacher. He was a guest speaker during a retreat when I was attending the Korean Baptist Church of Washington, located in Silver Spring, Maryland.

things of the world are a representation of God's goodness. Eating delicious food, sharing memorable moments with those we love, and appreciating the fun and interesting things of this world are reflections of all the good that God gives us.

But those things of the world, even if really good and sumptuous, can only go so far in helping us understand the unfathomable goodness of God, and too much of the good things of the world might prevent us from appreciating the Maker of those things. "If we don't feel strong desires for the manifestation of the glory of God, it is not because you have drunk deeply and are satisfied. It is because we have nibbled so long at the table of the world. Our soul is stuffed with small things, and there is no room for the great."[15] And besides hindering our ability to see God, having too much of a good thing often creates more difficulties and distractions in life too. Biggie Smalls observed this point in his posthumous number one single "Mo Money Mo Problems" when he laments that the more money he gains, the more problems come his way.[16]

If we somehow get to the point that the heart feels satisfied, there's still no peace, like when you eat sweets to answer a hungry stomach but then feel ill. "When a man desires a thing too much, he at once becomes ill at ease. . . . Yet if he satisfies his desires, remorse of conscience overwhelms him because he followed his passions and they did not lead to the peace he sought."[17]

Returning to the preacher at the church retreat who talked about the echoes of God's goodness, he continued by saying that even the vices of the world are just corruptions of those good things that should remind us of God's goodness to us. Alcoholism, drug abuse, prostitution, pornography, and overindulgence of pretty much anything else are degraded manipulations of things that are otherwise good. There's nothing bad about drugs to heal, sex to enjoy and procreate, and material things to experience, but we

---

15. Piper, *Hunger for God*, 25–26.

16. The Notorious B.I.G., "Mo Money Mo Problems," track 10 on *Life After Death*. If you're going to look up this song or listen to it, be warned that it has explicit lyrics!

17. à Kempis, *Imitation of Christ*, 6–7.

find ourselves in a really bad spot when we dive into those things trying to satisfy the longings in our eternal hearts. The bottomless heart will only want more drugs, more sex, more money—more of whatever you believe will fulfill you. The fifteenth century theologian Thomas à Kempis put it even more grimly: "A happy going often leads to a sad return, a merry evening to a mournful dawn. Thus, all carnal joy begins sweetly but in the end brings remorse and death."[18] Our faith must thus not rest on the seen things of this world to fill our hearts. Those things of the world don't provide the "*elegchos*," or proof,[19] of being able to fill our eternal hearts.

C. S. Lewis describes it like this:

> What Satan put into the heads of our remote ancestors was the idea that they could "be like gods"—could set up on their own as if they had created themselves—be their own masters—invent some sort of happiness for themselves outside God, apart from God. And out of that hopeless attempt has come nearly all that we call human history—money, poverty, ambition, war, prostitution, classes, empires, slavery—the long terrible story of many trying to find something other than God which will make him happy.
>
> The reason why it can never succeed is this. God made us: invented us as a man invents an engine. A car is made to run on petrol, and it would not run properly on anything else. Now God designed the human machine to run on himself.[20]

And that is what faith is: establishing a firm foundation for the eternal Being to fill up the eternity that he placed in our hearts to begin with. This in turn helps us find meaning in our lives. This is the kind of faith that led the centurion to ask Jesus just to "say the word" and not bother seeing the sick servant, being certain that Jesus could exercise his authority over all creation through a verbal command.

18. à Kempis, *Imitation of Christ*, 22.
19. See note 5 above. Yes, I'm mentioning a Greek word again here, but I promised not to dig up *new* Greek words.
20. Lewis, *Mere Christianity*, 49–50.

2

How Do We Obtain Faith?

THIS IS GOING TO sound discouraging, but I have to say it: faith is hard. Really hard. "Faith in God concerns the humanly impossible; it is literally *ridiculous* in its root meaning, from the Latin *ridere* (to laugh)."[1] However, notice that the quotation says it is *humanly* impossible to find and practice this faith on our own. We can still attain it with divine grace.

God Helps Us Attain Faith

It sounds paradoxical or perhaps tautological: God graciously gives us the ability to have faith in him. But it has to be true; we can't attain faith on our own.[2] We're too vulnerable to the enticing but empty promises of this world to fulfill our hearts, and the biggest reason for this is probably that we pursue only those things that we can actually see and understand, like money. This takes

---

1. Martin, *Between Heaven and Mirth*, 104 (emphasis in original; quoting Prof. Joseph Grassi's take on why Sarah laughed in Gen 18:12 upon hearing God's promise of a child at her very advanced age).

2. See, e.g., Rom 3:23 ("for all have sinned and fall short of the glory of God"); and Eph 2:8–9 ("For by grace you have been saved through faith. And this is not your own doing; it is the gift of God, not a result of works, so that no one may boast.")

us back to the definition of faith in Heb 11:1: "Now faith is the assurance of things hoped for, the conviction of things *not seen*."[3] Jonathan Edwards explained the situation plainly: "But the world did not see him."[4] How can you pursue something (or someone) you don't see?

There is a sadder and more important reason why faith in God is impossible through human effort alone. By our very nature, we are corrupted, imperfect beings who don't have the capacity to turn toward a perfect God. "The Lord looks down from heaven on the children of man, to see if there are any who understand, who seek after God. They have all turned aside; together they have become corrupt; there is none who does good, not even one."[5] The Apostle Paul recognized this very impediment to faith when he laments: "but I am of the flesh, sold under sin."[6] He continues by describing his discouraging fight against his natural state: "For I do not understand my own actions. For I do not do what I want, but I do the very thing I hate."[7] His carnal being, or his human-ness, just didn't have within itself the capacity to seek faith, and we're not any different from him. We're all human that way.

But there's good news: God desires to give us the grace that is needed for faith. He wants us to discover his unseen self.[8] And Pope John Paul II took it a step further by observing that God actually nudges us toward himself: "We begin to pray, believing that it is our own initiative that compels us to do so. Instead, we learn

---

3. Emphasis added. See also chapter 1, notes 1–5 above.

4. Edwards, *Religious Affections*, 4.

5. Ps 14:2–3. See also Isa 53:6 ("All we like sheep have gone astray we have turned—every one—to his own way"); and Rom 3:10–11 ("None is righteous, no, not one; no one understands; no one seeks for God. All have turned aside; together they have become worthless; no one does good, not even one.").

6. Rom 7:14. See also the verse in the King James Version ("but I am carnal, sold under sin").

7. Rom 7:15.

8. See, e.g., Jer 33:3 ("Call to me and I will answer you, and will tell you great and hidden things that you have not known.").

that it is always God's initiative within us, just as Saint Paul has written."[9]

Asking for a Desire to Have Faith

Some of us aren't at the point where we can have this faith—the belief that God can fill the eternity in our hearts. In that case, the *desire* to believe is a most important first step, and God can help us get there too. We need only ask.

There is a story in the Gospels of a boy who is possessed by an evil spirit.[10] He can no longer speak and suffers seizures, foaming at the mouth, and gnashing of the teeth. The boy's father takes him to see Jesus for a cure, and the father says, "[I]f you can do anything, have compassion on us and help us."[11] I'm gripped by how the father doesn't say, "Please have compassion on my son and help him." Instead, he asks Jesus to "have compassion on *us* and help *us*." The father is suffering just as much as his loving son is, and I can't imagine how he must feel to see his son like this.

Hearing the father's plea, Jesus challenges him in his reply, "'If you can'! All things are possible for one who believes." The father then exclaims, "I believe; help my unbelief!" The King James Version adds that the father cries out with tears as he says this.[12] What agony and anguish this father must feel wanting to believe for his son not to suffer anymore.

---

9. John Paul II, *Crossing the Threshold of Hope*, 17. The Pope's mention of what Saint Paul has written is in reference to Rom 8:26 ("Likewise the Spirit helps us in our weakness. For we do not know what to pray for as we ought, but the Spirit himself intercedes for us with groanings too deep for words.").

10. This story is recorded in Matt 17:14–18, Mark 9:14–27, and Luke 9:37–43. I'm drawing from the account in Mark.

11. Mark 9:22.

12. In the King James Version, Mark 9:24 reads, "And straightway the father of the child cried out, and said with tears, Lord, I believe; help thou mine unbelief."

Jesus then turns his attention to the evil spirit: "You mute and deaf spirit, I command you, come out of him and never enter him again."[13] The evil spirit then leaves the boy, and he is healed.

I was puzzled for a long time by what seems like the father's self-contradiction. He simultaneously tells Jesus that he believes and pleads for help with his unbelief. I would think that one would have one or the other. You can't believe and not believe at the same time.

Here's what I think is going on: None of the Gospel accounts say it, but I bet the father had tried everything for his son to be healed before going to Jesus. He probably went to multiple medical doctors, tried all kinds of folk remedies, and maybe even sought mediums to channel the supernatural. In any case, I'm sure he tried everything possible. He then heard of somebody named Jesus healing people of all kinds of maladies, and he thinks it's worth a shot. He finally reaches Jesus and tells him the situation about his son, but there is a storm raging in his heart: the father so desperately wants to believe that this Jesus can do something, but he can't. He has tried everything else, so why would this Jesus character be able to deliver?

The father hedges his bet and requests of Jesus: "*If* you can do anything, have compassion on us and help us." Jesus senses the lack of complete belief: "'*If* you can'! All things are possible for one who believes." Then the father cries out, "I believe; help my unbelief!" When he says he believes, he may not be believing completely but he is *willing himself* to get to the point of belief, and he's also asking Jesus to help him get to that point. In a way, the father is ordering himself to believe. It's like when we tell ourselves "I got this" when we're nervous and need to muster enough confidence to complete a difficult task successfully but we don't necessarily have enough of that self-confidence. For example, I tell myself "I got this" before delivering an important speech or briefing, while at bat in a softball game with the game-winning run on base, or even just trying to get my daughters to go to sleep at the end of the day when they're jumping around refusing even to get into bed.

13. Mark 9:25.

How Do We Obtain Faith?

But we have to remember that when it comes to faith in God, it is *humanly* impossible. Willing yourself to complete faith is not enough, and you have to ask God to help you reach it. In this story of the boy tormented by the evil spirit, I believe that after the father mustered as much faith as he could, God then helped him get over the last hump of unbelief in order to believe completely.

There is something else interesting about this story. Jesus, being God who knows all, must have known that the father did not have complete faith that his child could be healed. Instead of being critical of the father or even turning him away, Jesus encourages him by saying, "All things are possible for one who believes." He gives the father an opportunity to profess that he believes—or at least to profess that he believes as much as he can. At the same time, Jesus also allows the father to admit that he does not believe completely. God wants us to come to him and be honest even if our faith is lacking, and he is willing to help us expand our faith to be where it needs to be.

None of the three Gospel accounts states it explicitly, but I think the boy was healed because the father reached the point of believing completely that Jesus could do it. There are other stories in the Gospels of Jesus healing people *through* their faith. At the end of the story of the centurion, Jesus tells him, "Go; let it be done for you *as you have believed*," and the servant is said to have been "healed at that very moment."[14] When Jesus heals the bleeding woman[15] and the blind beggar,[16] he tells them, "Your faith has made you well." And when Jairus, the ruler of a synagogue, asks Jesus to heal his dying daughter, someone informs Jairus that his daughter has died and suggests not troubling Jesus anymore. But Jesus overhears this and tells Jairus: "Do not fear; only believe, and she will be well."[17] Jesus then brings the daughter back to life, and I believe the miracle came from Jesus through Jairus' faith.

14. Matt 8:13 (emphasis added).
15. Matt 9:22; Mark 5:34; and Luke 8:48.
16. Mark 10:52 and Luke 18:42.
17. Luke 8:50. This account also appears in Matt 9:18–26 (without recording Jesus' encouragement for Jairus only to believe) and Mark 5:36 (with an

In the same way, I am convinced that Jesus performed the miracle of driving the evil spirit out of the boy through the father's faith. The boy's father was able to will himself to a certain degree of faith, but not enough to save his son. God brought him the rest of the way, beyond what is humanly possible, to have enough faith for the boy to be healed.

Just a Little Bit of Faith Is Enough

This story should be an incredible encouragement to us. We need not possess a naturally unattainable amount of faith to find God. Rather, God will take however much we can marshal within ourselves and work with it. Jesus even says that he'll take faith as small as a mustard seed to do the impossible through us.[18] I didn't realize how small mustard seeds are until a few years ago when I went to a local grocery store with my daughter. I'd taught my daughter well because she told me we had to go to the back corner for the free samples. I've forgotten what foods they were giving out that day, but one of the samples had Dijon mustard applied on it. It tasted so good, so I bought a bottle of that mustard, which happened to be the kind with whole mustard seeds in it. When I was fixing myself a sandwich a few days later with that mustard, I noticed for the first time how tiny those seeds are.[19]

God will thus take the tiny speck of your faith and work with it to make it complete enough for him to fill the eternity in your heart. But there's a catch: even if your faith is the size of a mustard seed, it must represent 100 percent of all the faith that you can gather up within yourself. I shared some Bible verses earlier about how God will be there when we look for him,[20] but God has also

---

abridged version of the encouragement to believe).

18. Matt 17:20 ("For truly, I say to you, if you have faith like a grain of mustard seed, you will say to this mountain, 'Move from here to there,' and it will move, and nothing will be impossible for you.").

19. A mustard seed is 1 to 2 millimeters in diameter. See, e.g., Wikipedia, "Mustard Seed."

20. See note 8 above.

How Do We Obtain Faith?

said: "You will seek me and find me, when you seek me with *all your heart.*"[21]

To illustrate what this means, there is a story in the Gospels about a poor widow's offering.[22] Jesus and his disciples are hanging out at the temple and they see people making financial donations into the collection box. Many rich people are putting "large sums" into the box,[23] but then a poor widow comes along and puts in "two small copper coins," which the King James Version describes as "two mites." A mite was a Jewish coin that was the smallest denomination used in New Testament times and was worth 1/64 of a denarius.[24] A denarius was worth a day's wages at the time, so it is estimated that a mite was worth 1/8 of a cent today.[25] The poor widow's donation of two mites thus equates to 1/4 of one cent ($0.0025) in today's money—a most miniscule amount indeed.

Seeing the lady offer the two mites, Jesus calls his disciples over and says, "Truly, I say to you, this poor widow has put in more than all those who are contributing to the offering box. For they all

---

21. Jer 29:13 (emphasis added).
22. Mark 12:41–44. See also Luke 21:1–4.
23. Interestingly, the King James Version recounts that the rich people "cast" their large money into the offering box while the New International Version says they "threw" their monetary gifts into the box. The language reminds me of a road trip that I took to Chicago many years ago, and I came upon an unmanned toll booth that had a basket for collecting coins. I'd never seen a toll setup like that before, so I threw my coins overhand into the basket really hard. The coins went in but then all bounced out and onto the pavement below due to the excessive force of my throw. My juvenile mind is imagining the rich people throwing money into the box like that, but perhaps it's probably more accurate that they were tossing the money in there with an underhand throw. Regardless, I can't help but wonder why they threw the money in the box as opposed to gently placing the money in that box. Did they throw the money in for dramatic effect? Or perhaps they had some contempt at having to do the right thing? Whatever the case, I get the feeling that these rich people weren't giving with the right heart.
24. Taylor, "The Widow's Mite." The Greeks refer to the mite as a lepton, which is also what they call a euro cent today. Wikipedia, "Greek lepton."
25. Taylor, "The Widow's Mite."

contributed out of their abundance, but she out of her poverty has put in everything she had, all she had to live on."[26]

What faith the poor widow must have had to give all she had as an offering to the temple. How is she going to pay for her next meal? But that is the kind of faith required to find God. It doesn't have to be a lot—it can be as small as a mustard seed or 1/4 of a penny—but the little amount of faith that we gather up must constitute all of the faith we have. God will then work his grace to take us the rest of the way to the amount of faith needed to find fulfillment.

Admitting How Mucked Up We Are

Earlier, I said it's humanly impossible to believe God because we are corrupted beings.[27] There's yet another reason why it's so impossible: we usually don't own up to how corrupted we are. In order to obtain the faith we're talking about, there has to be an acknowledgment that we are in a rather hideous state, and we must thus plead with God for mercy. I believe this is why there are so many stories of Jesus healing terribly sick people. Those stories illustrate how awfully imperfect we are, and if we realized that, we'd be like the physically sick who go to God crying for healing.

The sick, paralyzed, demon-possessed, bleeding, blind, and leprous all had to recognize how desperately they needed his help before even thinking about going to Jesus. In a similar way, we need to recognize that in terms of spiritual health, we're all naturally in the same state as those whom Jesus healed—in dire need of serious help.[28] This is why Matthew refers to himself as "Matthew the tax collector," wanting to remind others that he was previously

---

26. Mark 12:43–44.

27. See nn. 5–7 above.

28. See, e.g., Ps 51:5 ("Behold, I was brought forth in iniquity, and in sin did my mother conceive me."); and Rom 3:23 ("for all have sinned and fall short of the glory of God").

How Do We Obtain Faith?

a scumbag who stole money by abusing his authority as a Roman taxman.[29]

People in the United States are not fond of the Internal Revenue Service and its agents today, and I imagine that the same ill sentiments fall on tax authorities all around the world. But the tax collectors in Jesus' day were on a wholly different level of repugnance. They shook down their own countrymen not just to collect taxes on behalf of the oppressive Roman Empire but also to pocket extra money from the taxpayers for themselves. The Romans authorized these taxmen to take from the conquered population however much they wanted for themselves after collecting the proper amount of taxes, and these traitors usually enriched themselves this way.[30]

We see evidence of this venality when John the Baptist tells tax collectors after baptizing them: "Collect no more than you are authorized to do."[31] We also see evidence of this kind of corruption when Zacchaeus promises to repay fourfold anyone he may have cheated through his work as a tax collector.[32]

The tax collectors are held in such low esteem that when Jesus first invited Matthew to a meal, the Pharisees[33] asked his disciples,

29. Matt 10:2–4 ("The names of the twelve apostles are these: first, Simon, who is called Peter, and Andrew his brother; James the son of Zebedee, and John his brother; Philip and Bartholomew; Thomas and Matthew the tax collector; James the son of Alphaeus, and Thaddaeus; Simon the Zealot, and Judas Iscariot, who betrayed him."). See also Manning, *Ragamuffin Gospel*, 138 (describing Matthew as "never wanting to forget who he was and always wanting to remember how low Jesus stooped to pick him up.").

30. *Life Application Study Bible (NIV)*, 1603, 1771; MacArthur, *Prodigal Son*, 15–16. For a further explanation of tax collectors and their practices during Jesus' day, see, e.g., Friedrichsen, "Temple, a Pharisee," notes 88–110.

31. Luke 3:13. As an aside, I find it interesting that John the Baptist didn't tell them to stop being tax collectors even though it was such a despised position in society. I take this to mean that as bad as it was to side treasonously with the Romans to collect taxes from one's fellow countrymen, that job in and of itself didn't amount to engaging in sin.

32. Luke 19:8.

33. A Pharisee was "a member of a Jewish sect of the intertestamental period [i.e., the period of time between the Old and New Testaments of the Bible] noted for strict observance of rites and ceremonies of the written law

"Why does your teacher eat with tax collectors and sinners?"[34] Tax collectors were such a disgrace and so loathed that they were classified apart from sinners in general. The tax collectors were mentioned separately: "tax collectors *and* sinners." That is the kind of reprobate that Matthew acknowledges himself to have been, and he doesn't want anybody to forget it.

Going back to the story of the centurion in the introduction to this book, he also knew he did not deserve to be in God's presence, so he told Jesus: "Lord, I am not worthy to have you come under my roof, but only say the word, and my servant will be healed."[35] This statement will sound familiar to our Catholic friends who celebrate mass. They say almost the exact same thing during communion after the priest presents the sacramental bread: "Lord, I am not worthy that you should enter under my roof, but only say the word and my soul shall be healed."[36] As they prepare to receive that sacramental bread, they tell God (and remind themselves) that they are indeed hopelessly contaminated by sin, just as the centurion did before Jesus granted his request for the servant to be healed. This is an important parallel, which a commentary on this Catholic liturgy emphasizes by stating: "Jesus works the cure because the centurion's humility overrides any other sinful condition. We [i.e., those partaking in communion] are imitating his humility, so that Jesus will not avoid us because of our sins."[37]

Thus, acknowledging how lowly we are is a very important element of faith. We won't feel a need to go to God unless we acknowledge the impurities in our lives, which if left unchecked lead us to the inadequate things of the world that falsely promise to satisfy us fully. "A person has to be thoroughly disgusted with the way things are to find the motivation to set out on the Christian

---

and for insistence on the validity of their own oral traditions concerning the law." Merriam-Webster, "Pharisee."

34. Matt 9:11.

35. Matt 8:8. See also Luke 7:6.

36. International Commission on English in the Liturgy, *Roman Missal*, 669.

37. Turner, *Understanding the Revised Mass Texts*, 60.

How Do We Obtain Faith?

way. . . . A person has to get fed up with the ways of the world before he, before she, acquires an appetite for the world of grace."[38] In that context, here's one more Gospel story about a dishonorable tax collector to drive the point home:

> [Jesus] also told this parable to some who trusted in themselves that they were righteous, and treated others with contempt: "Two men went up into the temple to pray, one a Pharisee and the other a tax collector. The Pharisee, standing by himself, prayed thus: 'God, I thank you that I am not like other men, extortioners, unjust, adulterers, or even like this tax collector. I fast twice a week; I give tithes of all that I get.' But the tax collector, standing far off, would not even lift up his eyes to heaven, but beat his breast, saying, 'God, be merciful to me, a sinner!' I tell you, this man went down to his house justified, rather than the other. For everyone who exalts himself will be humbled, but the one who humbles himself will be exalted."[39]

If he existed in real life, the tax collector in this parable probably shook a lot of money out of people, and I'm sure he would have spent the money on a big mansion, the equivalent of some luxury imported cars (maybe luxury imported chariots?), and the finest clothes. I also imagine he dined on the choicest meals and was perhaps a member of that society's version of a posh country club. But I'm guessing that it all left him empty, and it gnawed at him until somewhere along the way he realized what kind of scum he was for robbing money from others to fund his extravagance. He was fed up with the ways of the world and instead wanted grace in his life.

A Conscious Decision

At that point, a conscious decision is required to own up to the evil within ourselves just like that tax collector.[40] This is going to

---

38. Peterson, *Long Obedience*, 25.
39. Luke 18:9–14.
40. This conscious decision will also be needed during difficult moments in life to maintain faith in God. See chapter 3, note 9 below.

be difficult for most of us. I imagine that most of us aren't thieves, murderers, and certainly not Matthew's breed of tax collectors. However, we're really not that different from the more serious variety of sinners even if our own transgressions don't amount to felonies.

In fact, a leading expert on predicting violent behavior goes even further. In his book, *The Gift of Fear*, Gavin de Becker encourages his readers to trust their instincts and intuition to protect themselves from becoming victims of violent encounters like murders, rapes, and muggings. To help trust our instincts and intuition, he repeatedly makes the uncomfortable observation that "we have much more in common [with violent criminals] than we have in contrast."[41] In support of this argument, he notes that we are all capable of imagining the most despicable of actions that can be inflicted on another human being, so everyone possesses the necessary elements of a criminal mind. And although violent actions are rightfully considered repugnant, we cannot consider them inhuman. He ties this point to the overriding message of his book about how to avoid becoming a victim of violence: "To really work toward prediction and prevention [of violence], we must accept that these acts are done by people included in the 'we' of humanity, not by interlopers who somehow sneaked in."[42]

We are thus not too different from people like the corrupt tax collector (or worse), and we need to arrive at the same place as he did in asking God for mercy in the middle of the temple. That is what Christians call "repentance."

"Repentance is not an emotion. It is not feeling sorry for your sins. It is a decision."[43] As emotional as the tax collector in Jesus' parable might seem publicly beating his breast, it was still a conscious decision on his part not to let pride get in the way of finally acknowledging that only God can give him meaning. Without such an acknowledgment of how things are, the author of the First Epistle of John describes the situation like this: "If we say we

---

41. de Becker, *Gift of Fear*, 47.
42. de Becker, *Gift of Fear*, 51–52.
43. Peterson, *Long Obedience*, 29.

have no sin, we deceive ourselves, and the truth is not in us. If we confess our sins, he is faithful and just to forgive us our sins and to cleanse us from all unrighteousness."[44]

Once we acknowledge our sinful state, there is still one more step before we attain the faith that fills the eternity in our hearts. Paradoxically, that step requires an exercise of faith—a faith that we can indeed be cleaned of the sin in our lives through Jesus. In our natural corrupted state, we can't approach God because he is pure,[45] but Jesus took upon himself the penalty that we deserve to pay for having obeyed our carnal desires: death. He died on our behalf.[46] If we indeed believe that Jesus paid that price for us, God adopts us as his children.[47] That's when God resides in us and truly fills the eternity in our hearts.[48]

It's interesting to note that when Jesus and those who followed him talked about adoption as God's children, such assertions were

---

44. 1 John 1:8–9.

45. See, e.g., Hab 1:13 ("You who are of purer eyes than to see evil and cannot look at wrong.").

46. John 3:16–17 ("For God so loved the world, that he gave his only Son, that whoever believes in him should not perish but have eternal life. For God did not send his Son into the world to condemn the world, but in order that the world might be saved through him."). See also 2 Cor 5:21 ("For our sake he made him to be sin who knew no sin, so that in him we might become the righteousness of God.").

47. See, e.g., John 1:12–13 ("But to all who did receive him, who believed in his name, he gave the right to become children of God, who were born, not of blood nor of the will of the flesh nor of the will of man, but of God."); and Gal 4:4–7 ("But when the fullness of time had come, God sent forth his Son, born of woman, born under the law, to redeem those who were under the law, so that we might receive adoption as sons. And because you are sons, God has sent the Spirit of his Son into our hearts, crying, 'Abba! Father!' So you are no longer a slave, but a son, and if a son, then an heir through God.").

48. See, e.g., 2 Cor 4:6–7 ("For God, who said, 'Let light shine out of darkness,' has shone in our hearts to give the light of the knowledge of the glory of God in the face of Jesus Christ. But we have this treasure in jars of clay, to show that the surpassing power belongs to God and not to us."); Gal 2:20 ("I have been crucified with Christ. It is no longer I who live, but Christ who lives in me. And the life I now live in the flesh I live by faith in the Son of God, who loved me and gave himself for me."); and Eph 3:19 ("that you may be filled with all the fullness of God.").

made during the Roman occupation of Israel. A legal scholar notes that the New Testament's description of God's adoption of believers runs parallel to the law of adoption under Roman law at the time:

> The profound truth of Roman adoption was that the adoptee was taken out of his previous state and was placed in a new relationship of son to his new father, his new paterfamilias [the head of a Roman family]. All his old debts were canceled, and in effect the adoptee started a new life as part of his new family.[49]

It's easy to see the parallel between the biblical description of what it means to be adopted as God's children and the Roman law of adoption that existed when the books of the New Testament were written. When God adopts us, our moral debts of sin are canceled as we start a new life as a member of God's family.

Overcoming the Final Hump

Before I conclude this chapter on how to attain faith that fulfills our hearts and amazes God, I'd like to drop a word of encouragement for those of us who have decided to seek God but can't overcome the final hump in really believing and finding a fulfilled heart. Perhaps some of us are pleading, "Help my unbelief!" Or perhaps some of us just want to believe but can't find the motivation to do so. Either way, it may be like God is absent in your search. However, there's something astoundingly deep to keep in mind:

> Yet the experience of absence does not mean the absence of experience. For example, the soldier in combat who, during a lull in the battle, steals a glance at his wife's picture tucked in his helmet, is more present to her at that moment in her absence than he is to the rifle that is present in his hands. Likewise, the poor in spirit perceive that religious experience and mystical "highs" are not the

---

49. Lyall, *Slaves, Citizens, Sons*, 83.

How Do We Obtain Faith?

goal of authentic prayer, rather the goal is communion with God.[50]

God is still present in the experience of his absence. And what's important is that we remain in touch (or in communion) with God even if we don't feel him. Just keep going to God as you are and be honest with him, or as Father John Chapman famously said: "Pray as you can, not as you cannot!"[51] I'll share my thoughts on this more in the next chapter, but the simple act of praying (or talking) to God even when we don't feel like it strengthens our faith.[52]

Indeed, that's when faith can be at its strongest: when all indications are that the object of your faith doesn't exist. I think that's what was meant by one of the entries in Pudd'nhead Wilson's New Calendar in Mark Twain's novel, *Following the Equator*: "There are those who scoff at the schoolboy, calling him frivolous and shallow: Yet it was the schoolboy who said 'Faith is believing what you know ain't so.'"[53] It can be really hard to gather enough faith to fill even a mustard seed, especially when you start thinking your faith in God is ill placed. However, even the desire to believe what doesn't seem to be true for the sake of attaining a miniscule amount of faith can lead to the God who satisfies the eternity in our hearts. "In the very search for faith an implicit faith is already present, and therefore the necessary condition for salvation is already satisfied."[54] We then have to keep at it to test and prove this implicit faith.[55]

---

50. Manning, *Ragamuffin Gospel*, 82.

51. He apparently said this so much that I can't pinpoint a good citation for it. It's all over the Internet if you search for him and his quotation, including his Wikipedia entry ("John Chapman (priest)"), which does not provide a citation for the quotation either.

52. See chapter 3, notes 9–18 below.

53. Twain, *Following the Equator*, 64.

54. Pope John Paul II, *Crossing the Threshold of Hope*, 193.

55. Remember "elegchos" ("proof, conviction") in the definition of "faith" in Heb 11:1? See chapter 1, note 5 above.

3

How Do We Maintain Faith?

I F ATTAINING FAITH IS hard, maintaining it might be even harder, especially when we hit the inevitable low points in life.

The Undulations of Life

As the fictional high-ranking demon Screwtape observes, all humans are prone to the "law of Undulation," which is "the repeated return to a level from which [people] repeatedly fall back, a series of troughs and peaks."[1] And undulation affects everything we do, not just faith in God.

It is important to remember that these undulations are natural to all humans; we all go through them.[2] A spectacular example in the Bible is King David, who was called a man after God's own heart.[3] His faith in God led him as a boy to meet the nine-foot-tall Goliath in battle and walk away in complete victory as his nation's

---

1. Lewis, *Screwtape Letters*, 37.

2. Screwtape also says:"[Undulations] are merely a natural phenomenon which will do us [demons] no good unless you make a good use of it." Lewis, *Screwtape Letters*, 38.

3. 1 Sam 13:14; Acts 13:22.

hero.[4] Later, we see David on a spiritual peak when he exclaims: "Oh how I love your law! It is my meditation all the day."[5]

Yet, this same man of faith wrote many psalms of lament about unfortunate turns in his life. Here's a sampling:

- "Save, O Lord, for the godly one is gone; for the faithful have vanished from among the children of man. Everyone utters lies to his neighbor; with flattering lips and a double heart they speak."[6]
- "How long, O Lord? Will you forget me forever? How long will you hide your face from me? How long must I take counsel in my soul and have sorrow in my heart all the day? How long shall my enemy be exalted over me?"[7]
- "My God, my God, why have you forsaken me? Why are you so far from saving me, from the words of my groaning? O my God, I cry by day, but you do not answer, and by night, but I find no rest."[8]

I think about the mental and spiritual anguish that led David to write such dramatic lyrics as, "Will you forget me forever?" and "Why have you forsaken me?" What's even more amazing to me is that these are all words from the "man after God's own heart," and his faith was truly shaken in those moments. These writings should help us be comfortable with the notion that even those with the strongest faith can experience the kind of undulation that makes us doubt whether God is really with us.

---

4. See 1 Sam 17. David's victory was indeed complete. After he slung the stone that struck Goliath's forehead, David stood over him, took the giant's own sword, and severed his head with it (1 Sam 17:51). They never taught that part when I attended Sunday school as a child, and my apologies if that description is too graphic. I'm just repeating what's in the Bible.
5. Ps 119:97.
6. Ps 12:1–2.
7. Ps 13:1–2.
8. Ps 22:1–2.

Going to God Even When We Don't Feel Like It

Yet, it should not escape us what David did when he felt that God abandoned him; he still went to God, telling him honestly what was on his mind as recorded in the Psalms. Much like the first time we turn to God in faith, it takes a conscious decision to continue going to him even when things are difficult.[9] In fact, we have to push ourselves to turn to God in faith more often than not. The late pastor Eugene Peterson laid it down like this: "I have put great emphasis on the fact that Christians worship because they want to, not because they are forced to. But I have never said that we worship because we *feel* like it. Feelings are great liars. If Christians worshiped only when they felt like it, there would be precious little worship.... [W]e can *act* ourselves into a new way of feeling much quicker than we can *feel* ourselves into a new way of acting."[10]

When we will ourselves to turn to God even while we're in the troughs, that very act summons something powerful that helps us draw nearer to him. It's evident in the songs of lament, which begin with sorrowful verses but end with faith and hope.[11] Among the three examples of psalms of lament above, they turn more upbeat:

- "You, O Lord, will keep them; you will guard us from this generation forever."[12]
- "But I have trusted in your steadfast love; my heart shall rejoice in your salvation. I will sing to the Lord, because he has dealt bountifully with me."[13]

---

9. See chapter 2, note 40 above.

10. Peterson, *Long Obedience*, 54 (emphases in original).

11. Credit for this observation about how the psalms of lament lead to hope and how we should honestly tell God how we feel when things are difficult belongs to Pastor Dwight Yoo at Renewal Presbyterian Church in Philadelphia. I heard him preach about this on a Sunday morning, but I don't remember the date or even the year.

12. Ps 12:7. See note 6 above.

13. Ps 13:5–6. See note 7 above.

- "For he has not despised or abhorred the affliction of the afflicted, and he has not hidden his face from him, but has heard, when he cried to him."[14]

Laying our burdens before God necessarily brings us closer to him, just as people in the Gospels physically went to Jesus for healing. Indeed, God wants us to cast our burdens on him,[15] and he works through life's deep valleys to strengthen our faith.[16]

Our demonic friend Screwtape disgustedly says: "It is during such trough periods, much more than during the peak periods, that [a human] is growing into the sort of creature God wants [the human] to be. Hence the prayers offered in the state of dryness are those which please him best."[17] Screwtape understands how it works: difficult seasons in life can help us become the people whom God intended us to be by leading us to ask for the eternity established in our hearts to be filled. In his classic dramatic style, Jonathan Edwards said this about pulling through tough times with faith intact: "True virtue is loveliest when it is oppressed. The divine excellency of real Christianity is best exhibited when it is under the greatest trials."[18] With God's help, the key is to keep moving forward toward him when we're in our travails.

The First Easter

Perhaps the lowest of the lows that anybody felt in the Bible was on the very first Easter when Jesus' followers found that his remains

---

14. Ps 22:24. See note 8 above.

15. Matt 11:28 ("Come to me, all who labor and are heavy laden, and I will give you rest."); and 1 Pet 5:7 ("casting all your anxieties on him, because he cares for you."). See also the conclusion of another psalm of lament: Ps 55:22 ("Cast your burden on the Lord, and he will sustain you; he will never permit the righteous to be moved.").

16. See Jas 1:2–3 ("Count it all joy, my brothers, when you meet trials of various kinds, for you know that the testing of your faith produces steadfastness.").

17. Lewis, *Screwtape Letters*, 40.

18. Edwards, *Religious Affections*, 3.

were missing from the tomb.[19] These days, the church celebrates Easter every year as a reflection of hope for mankind made possible with the resurrection of Jesus, but it felt like the end of the world to Mary Magdalene and others when they saw the tomb empty.[20] The people who saw the empty tomb that Sunday morning had taken part in Jesus' ministry for so many years, sharing life with him and witnessing his miracles. Just one week earlier, Jesus had ridden into Jerusalem to throngs of people welcoming him as their king.[21] Now, Jesus was dead, and his remains were missing when his friends visited the tomb. Mary Magdalene "wept,"[22] and another account says that "trembling and astonishment had seized" the women who first saw the empty tomb and "fled" from it, telling nobody about what they saw (or didn't see) because they were so afraid.[23] In their dismay and shock, they'd forgotten about Jesus' prior promise to be back after death.[24] All they knew was that their teacher and friend was gone, and they probably felt that everything they did with Jesus all those years was in vain. The feeling of loss and even abandonment must have crushed their souls.

But Jesus was alive and many saw him during the course of that day and following week.[25] And after he showed himself to the

19. Matt 28:1–10; Mark 16:1–8; Luke 24:1–12; and John 20:1–8.

20. Credit for these insights about the first Easter goes to Pastor David Chang, who preached on this topic on April 12, 2020, at the church I currently attend: Open Door Presbyterian Church in Herndon, Virginia. I'm surprisingly able to recall the date of this sermon because I remember the sermon was delivered through a virtual broadcast on Easter Sunday at the beginning of the COVID-19 pandemic.

21. Matt 21:1–11; Mark 11:1–11; Luke 19:28–40; and John 12:12–19.

22. John 20:11.

23. Mark 16:8.

24. See, e.g., Matt 16:21 ("From that time Jesus began to show his disciples that he must go to Jerusalem and suffer many things from the elders and chief priests and scribes, and be killed, and on the third day be raised.").

25. The first person who saw Jesus was Mary Magdalene, but she thought that he was the gardener (John 20:15). This harkens back to the Garden of Eden, when Adam and Eve's job was essentially to be gardeners taking care of the world before sin entered it. Gen 2:15 ("The Lord God took the man and put him in the garden of Eden to work it and keep it."). This is a foreshadowing of

How Do We Maintain Faith?

disciples, he then told them to go into all the world and preach this good news of how God can save us and give meaning to our lives.[26] And that's exactly what they did. The book of Acts is littered with stories of the disciples healing people as Jesus did and speaking to thousands upon thousands, and they traveled as far and wide as modern-day Russia, Tunisia, Ethiopia, and India.[27] I believe that the disciples were able to engage in such amazing exploits because their faith was so severely tested between that first Good Friday and Easter.

I have a close friend dating back to middle school whose parents immigrated to the United States from the state of Kerala in India. The Orthodox church in which his family has worshiped is counted among the various churches and denominations in Kerala that are part of what is called the St. Thomas Christian community. The churches in that community trace their roots to the evangelistic work of Thomas the Apostle, and my exposure to that buddy's church has led me to have a deeper interest in that disciple.

There was one memorable conversation I had with my friend's father that solidified Thomas' standing as my favorite of the 12 disciples. When I was visiting his parents' house one day, one of the conversations turned to the story of Thomas, who is often derided as "doubting Thomas" for demanding proof it was really Jesus when he heard that he was back from the dead.[28] My friend's dad acknowledged that Thomas indeed doubted, but he added that what ultimately sets Thomas apart from the others was not his doubting but his subsequent unequivocal profession of faith. After seeing Jesus, Thomas exclaims, "My Lord and my God!"[29] None of the other disciples expressed their faith so strongly after seeing

---

Jesus beginning his work of restoration to bring things back to the way things were meant to be in the Garden of Eden. See Wright, *Surprised by Hope*, 210. In that light, it makes sense when the Apostle Paul describes Jesus as "the last Adam." See 1 Cor 15:45–49.

26. Mark 16:15 ("And he said to them, 'Go into all the world and proclaim the gospel to the whole creation.'").

27. Curtis, "Whatever Happened to the Twelve Apostles?"

28. John 20:25.

29. John 20:28.

Jesus, and perhaps Thomas was able to do so because his initial doubt had been deeper than that of the others.

Backtracking

Besides bad things that happen to us and make us feel discouraged, another type of natural undulation in life is being enticed to go back to the empty things of this world that promise to fill our hearts. When we turn toward God to fulfill our hearts, the things that we previously sought for the same purpose unfortunately don't just disappear. They're still around, and it can be really hard to resist the temptation to go back to our old ways. It's like people who quit smoking or drinking, but they'll still see cigarettes and alcohol in the store, on TV, and everywhere else. I understand that some former smokers and alcoholics who have gone clean for years will still be tempted even when they see somebody simply taking a drag on a cigarette or downing a pint.

Much like asking God to overcome our unbelief, maintaining faith consists of repeatedly doing our best to keep turning from those things that promise to do what only God can do, and we need to ask him continually to help us overcome any lack of faith that he is infinitely better than anything this world has to offer. It is a constant battle, and the scary thing is that when we slip into smaller enticements, it becomes harder and harder to resist when those enticements ramp up their assaults on our hearts. The very first Psalm illustrates what this looks like: "Blessed is the man who walks not in the counsel of the wicked, nor stands in the way of sinners, nor sits in the seat of scoffers."[30] There is a progression (or regression) in this Psalm: a person can begin by *walking* with bad company; he then stops and is *standing* with them; and finally, he makes himself comfortable by *sitting* with them.[31] The psalm is

---

30. Ps 1:1. Credit for the insight from this Psalm goes to my pastor for many, many years, Pastor Tony Chung, who was the head pastor of Grace Community Church of Silver Spring (Maryland).

31. See Boice, *Psalms*, 1:16 (observing Ps 1:1 as showing that "the way of the wicked is downhill and that sinners always go from bad to worse.").

saying that we need to keep moving past those things (or people) that call out to us in hopes of leading us astray from God, or else sin ensnares us and we get more and more rooted in the sin.

Of course, it's impossible to turn on our own from those secular things that keep calling out to us with their allure of fulfillment,[32] but we need to rely on God to get us over that final hump like the man asking for help in overcoming his unbelief.[33] God will give us what we need to resist those temptations.[34] Again, it's not very different from first attaining faith as discussed in chapter 2; it's just that now we have to keep looking to God repeatedly for our faith to reach its full measure.

The Higher You Fly the Harder You Fall

I don't want to be a downer, but realistically speaking, we're going to fall away from God. However, we can return to God even if we fall into the deepest of troughs in our undulations. It doesn't matter how hideous the sin is. Look at David: As high as his peaks were, David's troughs were truly abysmal. The worst of them was his affair with Bathsheba.[35] In fact, the affair is the one blot on his record: "David did what was right in the eyes of the Lord and did not turn aside from anything that he commanded him all the days of his life, except in the matter of Uriah the Hittite [Bathsheba's husband]."[36]

One evening, David sees from his rooftop a woman bathing, and the Bible describes her as "very beautiful." David orders somebody to track her down, and it is discovered that she is the wife of Uriah the Hittite, who happens to be not only a loyal soldier but one of the chiefs of David's "Mighty Men."[37]

---

32. See chapter 2, note 1 above regarding how faith is humanly impossible.
33. See chapter 2, note 12 above.
34. See, e.g., Phil 4:19 ("And my God will supply every need of yours according to his riches in glory in Christ Jesus.").
35. 2 Sam 11.
36. 1 Kgs 15:5.
37. 2 Sam 23:39; and 1 Chr 11:10, 41.

The Mighty Men are described as those "who gave [David] strong support in his kingdom, together with all Israel, to make him king."[38] There are incredible stories of their exploits, like the one who killed 800 of the enemy in battle by himself, or another whose hand "froze to the sword" when he was the only one to fight the enemy after everyone else retreated, or another who "went down into a pit on a snowy day and killed a lion."[39] I'm thinking that Uriah must have performed similar perilous and heroic feats to be one of the chiefs of the Mighty Men, all in service to David his king.

That doesn't stop David from summoning Uriah's wife and sleeping with her. As if that weren't bad enough, when Bathsheba informs David she is pregnant with his child, he covers it up by arranging for her husband Uriah to be killed on the battlefield. David then marries Bathsheba, and the Bible reports: "But the thing David had done displeased the Lord."[40]

Later, the prophet Nathan finds David and tells him to his face that what he did was wrong, but the prophet confronts him in a most dramatic way.[41] The prophet tells David a story about a poor man with a lamb that is like a part of his family after having grown up with his children. The lamb partakes in the family meals, drinks from the poor man's cup, and even sleeps in his arms. Meanwhile, a rich man doesn't want to take one of his own cattle or sheep to serve some guests a meal, so he steals the poor man's lamb and serves it as the meal for his guests. Upon hearing this, David erupts in anger and says the rich man deserves death and must pay for the lamb four times over. Nathan then says, "You are the man!"

---

38. 1 Chr 11:10.

39. 2 Sam 23:8–39. Regarding the one whose hand "froze to the sword," that description is from the New International Version. Other versions say that his hand "clung" (English Standard Version) and "clave" (King James Version) to the sword.

40. 2 Sam 11:27.

41. 2 Sam 12.

How Do We Maintain Faith?

David admits his wrongdoing and meekly says, "I have sinned against the Lord." And then something startling happens: Nathan informs David that the Lord "has put away your sin; you shall not die."[42] Just like that, he is back on God's good side. And the same is true for us: if we fall away from God, he will always take us back after we acknowledge our sin of letting something else take the place of God in our hearts. He'll take us back even if we steal another person's spouse and commit murder. (And remember, we're all capable of adultery, murder, and worse.)[43]

I can't overlook the fact that the end of this story isn't completely happy. Because of David's grievous sins of adultery and murder, the Bible says that God "afflicted" the baby he had with Bathsheba,[44] and the baby became sick and later died. These are very difficult developments to swallow, namely why an innocent baby boy needs to pay with his life for the sins of his father. But one thing we need to keep in mind is that the Old Testament law's punishment for both adultery and murder was death.[45] That's why when David admits to his wrongdoing, Nathan says not only that God has taken away his sin, but also that David won't die.[46] However, "even when sin is forgiven a price must be paid.... Often an innocent party pays the price of forgiveness."[47] Someone had to pay the death penalty that David deserved under the law for his transgressions.

Today, a basic tenet of Christianity would apply in such a situation: God in the form of a person died the death that we deserve and overcame the ultimate penalty through his resurrection.[48] Jesus is the innocent person who paid the price for our

---

42. 2 Sam 12:13.

43. See chapter 2, notes 41–42 above.

44. 2 Sam 12:15. The King James Version and New International Version say that God "struck" the child.

45. See Lev 20:10 and Deut 22:22 (regarding adultery); and Lev 24:17 (regarding murder).

46. See note 42 above.

47. Guzik, "2 Samuel 12."

48. See chapter 2, notes 45–48 above.

31

transgressions. This is why when John sees Jesus, he proclaims, "Behold, the Lamb of God, who takes away the sin of the world!"[49] The wages of sin is death,[50] but the work of this Lamb of God allows us access to God, which was graphically illustrated when at the very moment that Jesus died on the cross, "the curtain of the temple was torn in two, from top to bottom."[51] Up to that point, only the high priest could venture beyond that curtain, which he did only once per year with the blood of an animal sacrifice for the sins of the people.[52] But now that the curtain was torn away, we can all freely approach God without a blood sacrifice for our sins, for Jesus the Lamb paid the ultimate sacrifice with his blood to cover our wages of sin.[53] The Apostle Paul summed it up well: "But now in Christ Jesus you who once were far off have been brought near by the blood of Christ."[54]

Returning to David, God ends up taking David back. David and Bathsheba have another son, Solomon,[55] who ends up being not only another great king in his own right but is also a direct ancestor of Jesus himself. However, the account of Jesus' genealogy won't let the reader forget what happened: "And David was the father of Solomon *by the wife of Uriah.*"[56] I believe that this remark is in the genealogy not so much to draw attention to David's awful lapse in judgment that led to adultery and murder, but the intent is to show the extent of God's grace: no sin is too big for God's grace to overcome.

---

49. John 1:29.

50. Rom 6:23.

51. Matt 27:51.

52. Moses' brother, Aaron, performed the first sacrifice on the day of atonement as God instructed in Lev 16, and this annual sacrifice continued through Jesus' day as described in Heb 9:1–9.

53. Heb 9:9–28.

54. Eph 2:13.

55. 2 Sam 12:24.

56. Matt 1:6 (emphasis added).

How Do We Maintain Faith?

Getting Back Up Like the Prodigal Son

The important point here is that there is always a way back to God even after falling for something that promises to take the place of God in our hearts, and this includes committing the most serious offenses. A striking illustration of this point is Jesus' parable of the prodigal son.[57] A wealthy man had two sons, and the younger son asked his father for his share of the estate. The father gave the younger son his share, and the young man went to a distant country and "squandered his property in reckless living." He spent absolutely everything, and the timing couldn't be any worse because a severe famine had begun just then. The prodigal son was in a really bad spot.

A citizen of that country hired him to feed pigs, but the prodigal son still didn't earn enough to have enough to eat. His circumstances had become so dire that "he was longing to be fed with the pods that the pigs ate, and no one gave him anything." He then realized that at least his father's hired hands had enough to eat, so he planned to go back to his father. He prepared a speech to his father to admit that he sinned against him and to beg to be hired as a servant.

As he approached home, his father saw him a long ways off and ran to him and then hugged and kissed him. The son began his planned speech acknowledging his sin and begging for a job, but he couldn't finish because the father ordered the servants to clothe his son with the best robe, put shoes on his feet, place a ring on his finger, and slaughter the fatted calf for a feast. After the feast had started, the older son approached the house after working in the field. When he saw what was happening, he became very angry and refused to join the feast. He complained bitterly to his father that while he served him and never disobeyed him for so many years, his younger brother was enjoying a feast after he squandered his share of the property on prostitutes. The father replied, "Son, you are always with me, and all that is mine is yours. It was fitting

---

57. Luke 15:11–32.

to celebrate and be glad, for this your brother was dead, and is alive; he was lost, and is found."

The Context of the Parable of the Prodigal Son

This parable is a wonderful story of forgiveness and restoration, but we most likely do not grasp its full depth because of our lack of familiarity with the cultural and societal context of the story. We need to understand that context to appreciate the humiliation and shame that the father assumed for the prodigal son to be welcomed back into the family. The magnitude of the father's forgiveness for the prodigal son was truly unfathomable to the sinners, tax collectors, Pharisees, and everybody else who may have been listening to this parable in the first-century Middle East.

All indications from the parable itself are that the father was not just rich, but he was an immensely wealthy man of very high social standing. His property was enormous, evidenced by the fact that the older son didn't know about the feast until he was returning home after working in the distant fields. Feasts like the one that the father threw in this story were absolutely buzzing, loud, and even raucous with professional music and merriment, and the sound of the music would easily have carried over half a mile.[58] The older son must have been very far away indeed not to hear the noise from the feast, but he was still on his father's property even at such a long distance from home. Even in the present day, it's usually only the most wealthy who own such vast amounts of good land. I imagine the father of the parable must have been the wealthiest of the wealthy to own so much land in those days.

The younger son's demand for his share of the inheritance was deeply offensive, unconscionable, and most dishonoring to the father. This was even more so because he was so young; he was probably a teenager because he was unmarried.[59] Even today, could you imagine a young man not just requesting but demanding

---

58. MacArthur, *Prodigal Son*, 156.
59. *ESV Study Bible*, 1989.

that his mom and dad give him his inheritance immediately? It would indeed be shameful.[60] Furthermore, established laws and customs at the time governed the passage of family estates. There was a legal procedure for the father to divide his property among his sons as his death approached, which would grant the sons legal right of possession but not disposition.[61] In other words, the sons would own shares of the father's land but not the right to control and expend the property. By expressing the desire for his share of his inheritance, the prodigal son was implying his wish that his father be dead.[62] As a consequence of violating his father's honor, the expected and proper reaction according to those listening to this parable would have been for the father to beat the son or perhaps arrange for his execution by stoning. That is what the law of the time commanded for a hopelessly stubborn and rebellious child.[63]

Shockingly to Jesus' audience, the father did none of those things and gave the abhorrent son what he wanted, which must have amounted to an enormous mass of wealth. Those listening to the parable—especially the religious teachers and leaders—would have heaped scorn on the father for allowing this spoiled and repugnant young man to avoid any of the consequences that he

---

60. See also *Life Application Study Bible (NIV)*, 1764 (describing the younger son's initiation of the division of the estate as "arrogant disregard for his father's authority as head of the family."); Bailey, *The Cross and the Prodigal*, 41 ("Does any culture anywhere condone such a request?").

61. Bailey, *Cross and the Prodigal*, 41.

62. MacArthur, *Prodigal Son*, 44–45. See also Bailey, *Cross and the Prodigal*, 41 (recounting the author's travels throughout the Arab world asking whether a son could ever make such a request of the father with the invariable answer that it would never happen because the request would mean that the son wants the father to die).

63. MacArthur, *Prodigal Son*, 46. Deut 21:18–21 provides: "If a man has a stubborn and rebellious son who will not obey the voice of his father or the voice of his mother, and, though they discipline him, will not listen to them, then his father and his mother shall take hold of him and bring him out to the elders of his city at the gate of the place where he lives, and they shall say to the elders of his city, 'This our son is stubborn and rebellious; he will not obey our voice; he is a glutton and a drunkard.' Then all the men of the city shall stone him to death with stones. So you shall purge the evil from your midst, and all Israel shall hear, and fear."

deserved. But the audience will be even more aghast by the father later in the story.

Wild Living and Returning Home in Shame

The younger son went to a distant country and "squandered his property in reckless living." The King James Version says that he "wasted his substance with riotous living." Words like "reckless" and "riotous" suggest that this young man engaged in all kinds of illicit activity to feed his carnal desires, which included prostitutes according to his older brother's statements later in the parable. However, some believe that the prodigal son didn't really engage in illicit activity but rather unwisely spent his fortune trying to make friends by throwing banquets and giving gifts.[64] Regardless of what he did exactly, the younger son squandered his entire inheritance. All. Of. It.

Just then, a famine arrived in that country, and he found a job feeding pigs to survive. As one might imagine, the job had to have been quite dirty. And for the Jewish listeners of this story, they would have been troubled for deeper reasons: under their religious law, pigs were considered unclean animals.[65] The prodigal son was in contact with the swine every day, and as one Bible commentary says, the audience hearing this parable would have considered this young man to be "degraded beyond belief."[66]

Things got so bad that the prodigal entertained the thought of eating the pig feed, but then he finally came to his senses. His father was an honorable man who treated his servants well; the prodigal would be much better off being his father's hired hand than trying to eke out an existence feeding pigs. So he decided to go back home, and he prepared a speech for his father: "Father, I

---

64. See, e.g., Bailey, *Cross and the Prodigal*, 53–54.

65. Lev 11:7.

66. *Life Application Study Bible (NIV)*, 1764. See also Stein, *New American Commentary*, 405 (describing the Prodigal Son as a "Jewish man on skid row" at this point in the parable).

have sinned against heaven and before you. I am no longer worthy to be called your son. Treat me as one of your hired servants."

When the prodigal son returned home, the extent of the father's mercy might have been for the son to work a lifetime to make up for his wrongs. This "son" had to pay for all the dishonor that he had dumped on his father and family, and it would have been within the father's right to arrange for the death of this son under the law.[67] Anything short of these repercussions would have been considered merciful.

Trading Shame for Restoration

The father did something that would have given the audience seizures and heart stress: while the son was still a long ways off, he *ran* to his son. In fact, the original Greek uses the technical word for running in athletic contests to describe how the father raced to his son.[68] A nobleman running would have been entirely unheard of in the first century Middle East, and the father in this parable would have had to pull up his robe to run, which was utterly undignified[69] and even described as "painfully shameful."[70] This scene is so explicitly and abhorrently shocking to the Middle Eastern mindset that Arabic translations of the Bible often describe the father's response with euphemisms saying that he "hurried" or "presented himself" to the prodigal son.[71] And as if running wasn't enough, the father then "embraced him and kissed him," and the King James Version says that he "fell on his neck, and kissed him."[72]

---

67. See note 63 above.

68. Bailey, *Cross and the Prodigal*, 67.

69. MacArthur, *Prodigal Son*, 113–14. See also *ESV Study Bible*, 1989 (stating: "The father cast aside all behavioral conventions of the time, as running was considered to be undignified for an older person, especially a wealthy landowner as this man.").

70. Bailey, *Cross and the Prodigal*, 67.

71. MacArthur, *Prodigal Son*, 113–14.

72. Luke 15:20. See *ESV Study Bible*, 1989 (stating that "embraced him" is literally "fell on his neck" in the original Greek).

When I was in high school and working at a church summer camp, a little girl was running around a playground with a Doritos chip in one hand when she tripped on something (maybe her own feet). As she was falling down, she held out that hand to the sky to protect the Doritos chip from breaking and getting dirty. After her body thumped onto the playground mulch, her clothes were sullied with dirt, but none of that mattered to the child. Her arm was still pointing straight up holding the precious Doritos chip, and the chip was safe, clean, and intact. The little girl was relieved, and I could tell that she thought it was worth sacrificing her body to save her precious triangular orange treat.

Similarly but of course more intensely, the young man meant everything to his father. The father was willing to harm and sully himself so that his son's life and dignity could remain safe, clean, and intact. By acting so shamefully in being the first to reach his son, the father was humbling himself in order to deflect any abuse targeted at the son.[73] Who could heap scorn on the son or raise a stone against him if his father has covered him in his embrace? Rather, any scorn would now go to the father: how could he act so shamefully? Why not let the son suffer what he deserves? But it gets even more outlandish in the eyes of Jesus' audience.

The son started his planned speech, but he only got to the part about not being worthy to be called a son before the father ordered his servants to clothe the prodigal son with the "best" robe, put a ring on his finger, and bring shoes for his feet. A nobleman's best robe was worn very rarely and only for the most special of occasions, perhaps for a firstborn's wedding; the ring signified the bearer's authority over the estate; and the shoes signified the son's restoration into the family, for hired hands and slaves went barefoot.[74]

---

73. The son would have been subject to an intense variety of abuse, for the traditional consequence for someone who squandered his entire inheritance like the son did was to be cut off from his community completely. Bailey, *Cross and the Prodigal*, 52–53.

74. MacArthur, *Prodigal Son*, 127–35. See also Bailey, *Cross and the Prodigal*, 70–71.

But wait, there's more! The father ordered that the fatted calf be slaughtered for a big feast. The fatted calf was kept apart from the rest of the herd, was fed the choicest grains for only the rarest of special occasions, and was most likely big enough for everybody in the banquet to have their fill of meat.[75] There were music and dancing, and there was surely a neverending flow of alcohol.[76]

Social Suicide

Can you imagine what the prodigal son must have been thinking at this point? He had contemplated eating pig feed in just the previous scene, and then he was going to eat a delectable fatted calf during a feast in his honor.[77] Looking around at the tremendous amount of merriment, the prodigal son may have thought to himself that his father was going to spend a lot of money to throw this lavish party. However, this feast cost the father much more than just money.

In the movie *Mean Girls*, Regina George warns Cady Heron not to join the Mathletes because doing so would be "social suicide" in their high school. None of their peers in the most popular echelons of the high school pecking order would continue associating with Cady if she became a member of perhaps the nerdiest of extracurricular groups. However, Cady at least retained some friends after becoming a Mathlete, even if they were the unpopular variety and her standing fell in the school's student body hierarchy. But when the prodigal son's father not only restored him into the family but also celebrated his return, he truly committed social suicide: he completely killed his own standing in the community. In a society where respect and shame meant vastly more than they do where I live today, the father took on the irredeemable indignity of his despicable son. And remember, the son did *nothing* to

---

75. MacArthur, *Prodigal Son*, 137–38.

76. Raucous parties often serve as an illustration of the kingdom of God and heaven. See the discussion on the kingdom of God being a party in chapter 4, notes 1–19 below.

77. Henry, *Commentary on the Whole Bible*, 1880.

make up for his grievous misdeeds. Yet, like the baby who died in lieu of David after his acts of adultery and murder,[78] the father paid the ultimate price socially that was due for the outrageous offenses of his younger son.

And let's not forget about the older son, who is often overlooked in this story. It's hard for most of us in the modern day to notice this, but it is important to know that the older son also greatly dishonored his father and that the father humiliated himself to show him grace too.[79] The societal mores of the time dictated that the older son enter the house and greet the guest of honor. By refusing to do so, the older son was making public his disapproval of the restoration of his younger brother and the ensuing feast, for everybody would have noticed his absence in the banquet. The older brother's open denunciation of his father's actions was a more serious offense than the younger son's earlier demand for his share of the inheritance, which was performed in private. Consequently, the father would have been expected to safeguard his honor by punishing the older son severely, but the father instead humiliated himself by leaving the banquet to present himself to the older son outside and plead for reconciliation with his younger brother. This would have absolutely stunned the guests of the banquet (and presumably those listening to the story too as Jesus was telling it). The father thus commits social suicide a second time in this story so that he could cover over the unforgiveable wrongs of the other son.

Likewise, God went to great lengths to allow us to approach him freely. He came down to earth, presented himself in the form of his own created humans, and then died a humiliating death at the hands of those corrupted creations.[80] Jesus endured it all so

---

78. See note 44 above.

79. The observations in this paragraph about the seriousness of the older son's disrespectful behavior and the magnitude of the father's humiliation in showing him grace is from Bailey, *Cross and the Prodigal*, 81–83.

80. See Phil 2:5–8 ("Have this mind among yourselves, which is yours in Christ Jesus, who, though he was in the form of God, did not count equality with God a thing to be grasped, but emptied himself, by taking the form of a servant, being born in the likeness of men. And being found in human form, he humbled himself by becoming obedient to the point of death, even death

that our sins won't prevent us from freely approaching God and establishing a real relationship with him. And like the prodigal son, if we own up to those things that lead our hearts astray, he is always willing to forgive and bring us back into his fold.[81] No matter how detestable our lives have been, we too will be given the special robe, ring, sandals, and fatted calf. This is how Brennan Manning describes the end result: "Whatever past achievements might bring us honor, whatever past disgraces might make us blush, all have been crucified with Christ and exist no more except in the deep recesses of eternity, where 'good is enhanced into glory and evil miraculously established as part of the greater good.'"[82]

A Healthy Sense of Fear and Awe

I think that God's ability to forgive all sins is one of the reasons why the Bible encourages us to fear the Lord.[83] It's one thing to wrong somebody and to receive forgiveness from that person. It is in the wronged person's authority to forgive because the sin was against that aggrieved person. But I can't come along as a third party and forgive the wrongdoer in that situation. I have no authority to do that because I wasn't wronged. With that illustration, we should begin seeing the enormity of what it means for God to forgive any and all sins across all time. If we try to imagine all the wrongs that each of us has committed in our lives, it would be beyond measure.

Now imagine the sheer volume of sins amassed among the more than 7 billion people on Earth today, and then think about the estimated 117 billion people who have ever lived.[84] Who has

---

on a cross.").

81. 1 John 1:9. See chapter 2, note 44 above.

82. Manning, *Ragamuffin Gospel*, 54 (partly quoting Tugwell, *Beatitudes*, 7).

83. See, e.g., Ps 111:10 ("The fear of the Lord is the beginning of wisdom; all those who practice it have a good understanding."); and Prov 14:27 ("The fear of the Lord is a fountain of life, that one may turn away from the snares of death.").

84. These population figures are from Kaneda and Haub, "How Many

the authority to forgive that imponderably massive volume of sin? It's in that context the psalmist wrote: "If you, O Lord, should mark iniquities, O Lord, who could stand? But with you there is forgiveness, *that you may be feared.*"[85] It might not be evident what it means for God to "mark equities," but perhaps it would help to look at the New International Version, which says: "If you, Lord, kept a record of sins."[86] Yes, God is to be feared because he can perform amazing miracles and can smite us if he wants, but only a most awesome power who has authority over everything can forgive all the recorded transgressions of all humankind. This should give us serious pause.

The word "awesome" is really abused and overused these days to the point that its meaning has been completely watered down. You had a big burrito for lunch today? Some people would hear that and say, "Awesome." Or you've read and seen all the books and movies in a long science fiction or fantasy adventure series? Like-minded fans may say you're "awesome" for doing that. Or you got tickets to the Super Bowl? "Awesome." No, those things are not awesome. They might be cool, noteworthy, or even great, but they're not awesome. As the dictionary defines it, "awesome" means "inspiring awe,"[87] and "awe" in turn means "an emotion variously combining dread, veneration, and wonder that is inspired by authority or by the sacred or sublime."[88]

People?"

85. Ps 130:3–4 (emphasis added).

86. The verse from the New International Version in full: "If you, Lord, kept a record of sins, Lord, who could stand? But with you there is forgiveness, so that we can, with reverence, serve you." You may notice that the New International Version does not use the word "fear" but instead says "with reverence, serve you," even though the previous edition of the New International Version from 1984 said "that you may be feared." However, the original term in the Hebrew is "fear." Strong, *New Exhaustive Concordance*, s.v. "אָרֵי" (Hebrew entry no. 3372). See also the verse in the King James Version: "But there is forgiveness with thee, that thou mayest be feared."

87. Merriam-Webster, "Awesome."

88. Merriam-Webster, "Awe."

How Do We Maintain Faith?

So you know what's awesome in the truer sense of the word? How about the Apostle John's encounter with Jesus as described in the Book of Revelation: "The hairs of [Jesus'] head were white, like white wool, like snow. His eyes were like a flame of fire, his feet were like burnished bronze, refined in a furnace, and his voice was like the roar of many waters. In his right hand he held seven stars, from his mouth came a sharp two-edged sword, and his face was like the sun shining in full strength."[89] Seeing this otherworldly appearance, John "fell at his feet as though dead."[90]

Indeed, something awesome should remind us of our mortality, like when people describe the horrors of surviving a major hurricane or earthquake. Or when a man encounters a 400-pound mama grizzly bear that attacks him with multiple bites measuring 1,000 PSI of pressure (which can crush bowling balls) and with paws that measure more than 9 inches wide and curved claws 5 inches long, but he somehow survives this beast of nature.[91] Or when I went to see a NASCAR race at Dover International Speedway in 2009, I saw Joey Logano's car roll more than seven times after crashing into other cars and the outer wall, and I thought he'd emerge severely maimed if not dead. But no, he leisurely climbed out of the wreckage and tipped his hat to the crowd while strolling to the waiting ambulance.[92]

Those are the kinds of moments when we feel true awe: when something with absolute force and authority bares our fragility and finiteness. And that is an apt description of the raw power of God, who instead of smiting us eradicates the sin of mankind that should lead to death for us all. That is truly *awesome*, and that is the kind of God who wants to dwell in our hearts.

---

89. Rev 1:14–16.

90. Rev 1:17.

91. Bennett, "Grizzly Hell." (Warning: there is a photo of the man's very bloody face after the bear attack.)

92. See, e.g., Spencer, "Joey Logano."

Being Aware of God's Wonders Around Us

I'd like to share about something that has helped me build my faith (or at least keep it from getting weaker): trying to seek out God's wonders around me. Sometimes, I'll drive to the mountains to hike through nature. Or when I'm outside in the evenings, I've made it a habit to look up into the sky at the stars that are unfathomably millions of light years away and at the planets of the solar system that race around the sun with our planet. One minister has said that his relationship with God totally changed when he "became a lover of nature. I loved it, not because of what it was and is, but for what came through it and what it could become to anyone who surrenders to its wonder."[93]

And it's not just in nature where I find reason to wonder. It's in the joy of watching my daughters play or learn something new. It's in the ingenuity and creativity that God has placed in us to be able to build high performance cars, construct incredibly tall skyscrapers, and compose beautiful music. It's also in a right fielder throwing a baseball like a cannon to get a runner out at third base, an engineer meticulously calculating the exact angle of entry needed for astronauts to return to Earth safely, and a skilled cook preparing a scrumptious meal. These incredible skills should remind us of the great works of God.

> By and large, our world has lost its sense of wonder.... Our world is saturated with grace, and the lurking presence of God is revealed not only in spirit but in matter—in a deer leaping across a meadow, in the flight of an eagle, in fire and water, in a rainbow after a summer storm, in a gentle doe streaking through a forest, in Beethoven's Ninth Symphony, in a child licking a chocolate ice cream cone, in a woman with windblown hair. God intended for us to discover his loving presence in the world around us.[94]

---

93. Campolo, *Carpe Diem*, 145.

94. Manning, *Ragamuffin Gospel*, 49. See also, e.g., Jas 1:17 ("Every good gift and every perfect gift is from above, coming down from the Father of lights, with whom there is no variation or shadow due to change.").

How Do We Maintain Faith?

I believe that God speaks to us through the wonders around us. Of course, it's harder for many of us to pick up on what God is saying through those wonders because we're so busy, and there's so much noise, and there is so much else vying for our attention. We need to make a conscious decision to take even a moment to stop and notice these wonders arounds us. Or perhaps we need to get away once in a while from our everyday lives and go somewhere quiet, for God's voice can be as small as a whisper.[95] And when we come across something wondrous, we can find a closer connection to God himself if we savor it.

Before Mary gave birth to Jesus, she met the angel Gabriel who told her about how divinely special her baby boy would be.[96] And when the shepherds paid a visit after Jesus was born, Mary saw a heavenly host singing praises to God. It is written that after she witnessed all these wonders, "Mary treasured up all these things, pondering them in her heart."[97] I think this is the most beautiful verse in the whole Bible. She treated what she witnessed as what they obviously were: wonders of God. She couldn't help but treasure them as experiences that no money can ever buy, and she pondered over them. What did she ponder? Maybe she wondered why God chose her to be the lucky recipient of such awe-inspiring events. Or maybe she contemplated the immense place in history

---

95. 1 Kgs 19:11–13 ("And he said, 'Go out and stand on the mount before the Lord.' And behold, the Lord passed by, and a great and strong wind tore the mountains and broke in pieces the rocks before the Lord, but the Lord was not in the wind. And after the wind an earthquake, but the Lord was not in the earthquake. And after the earthquake a fire, but the Lord was not in the fire. And after the fire the sound of a low whisper. And when Elijah heard it, he wrapped his face in his cloak and went out and stood at the entrance of the cave. And behold, there came a voice to him and said, 'What are you doing here, Elijah?'"). However, I'll acknowledge that there are also accounts of God speaking through a storm (Job 38:1) and through fire and earthquake simultaneously (Exod 19:18), and his voice is said to sound like thunder (1 Sam 2:10; John 12:28–29).

96. Luke 1:26–38.

97. Luke 2:19.

that she held as the mother of Jesus.[98] Whatever it was that went through her mind, Mary dwelled on these wonders.

Nature through its mystery and majesty points to the handiwork of God,[99] and the amazing handiwork of human hands and minds is a reflection of our special place on this earth as God's image bearers.[100] If we can take a moment to notice God reminding us of his love and greatness through nature and other wonders that we personally experience, and if we treasure up what we notice and ponder them, it will help us fathom a little better how God can fill our hearts.

---

98. When Mary was pregnant with Jesus, her friend Elizabeth tells her: "Blessed are you among women, and blessed is the fruit of your womb!" (Luke 1:42). Sensing the enormity of her place in history as Jesus' mother, Mary then says: "For behold, from now on all generations will call me blessed" (Luke 1:48).

99. See Job 12:7–10 ("But ask the beasts, and they will teach you; the birds of the heavens, and they will tell you; or the bushes of the earth, and they will teach you; and the fish of the sea will declare to you. Who among all these does not know that the hand of the Lord has done this? In his hand is the life of every living thing and the breath of all mankind."). See also Rom 1:20 ("For his invisible attributes, namely, his eternal power and divine nature, have been clearly perceived, ever since the creation of the world, in the things that have been made. So they are without excuse.").

100. Gen 1:26–27. See chapter 1, note 7 above.

4

Where Does Faith Lead?

IN CHAPTER 1, I shared that faith is being sure of what we hope for: that God would satisfy the eternity in our hearts and give meaning to us. In chapter 2, I delved into how we can achieve such faith. And in the previous chapter, I considered how to maintain such a faith even when so much of the world around us works against it. We now have to turn to a question of practicality: so what? If we achieve this amazing faith, what happens next and what can we do with it?

If we can feel that our hearts are satisfied after reaching out to God, that is fantastic. However, that won't mean anything if we keep it to ourselves. The centurion exhibited his amazing faith only through his care for another person. And like the centurion, we won't be able keep it to ourselves when we attain this faith. From our hearts will automatically flow joy, hope, and love, the last of which includes a desire for justice to the downtrodden.

Joy

"Joy is the most infallible sign of the presence of God."[1] This is probably why there are so many commands in the Bible for us to

---

1. Martin, *Between Heaven and Mirth*, 15 (quoting Jesuit priest Teilhard

have joy or to rejoice.[2] If God is indeed residing in our hearts, we should not be able to help but show joy. Tony Campolo goes so far as to say that the kingdom of God is a party, which makes sense because a party is what you get when joyful people gather.

Pastor Campolo has written a book with actually that title, *The Kingdom of God Is a Party*, in which he makes an astounding observation about one of the tithes in the Old Testament.[3] These days, churchgoers are encouraged (and often commanded) to give a tithe, or 10 percent of their income, to their church for its operations and ministries. But in Old Testament times, there were three types of tithes:[4] (1) 10 percent of one's firstfruits and firstlings every year to support the priests who work at the temple;[5] (2) 10 percent of all that one's fields produce each year for the feasts;[6] and (3) 10 percent from the produce of every third year for the poor.[7] Pastor Campolo zeroed in on the second type of tithe: the one for the feasts, which upon closer reading isn't used for something that most would consider "holy." It was to be expended for a huge party every year.

The Lord commanded the Israelites to eat and drink a tenth of their harvest, wine, oil, and firstborn of their herd and flock at a place he would choose. And if they couldn't carry everything to that appointed place, the Lord further commanded the Israelites as follows: "then you shall turn [the harvest, wine, oil, etc.] into money and bind up the money in your hand and go to the place that the Lord your God chooses and spend the money for whatever

---

de Chardin).

2. See, e.g., Ps 32:11 ("Be glad in the Lord, and rejoice, O righteous, and shout for joy, all you upright in heart!"); and Phil 4:4 ("Rejoice in the Lord always; again I will say, rejoice."). See also 1 Thess 5:16–18 ("Rejoice always, pray without ceasing, give thanks in all circumstances; for this is the will of God in Christ Jesus for you."). I don't think it's a coincidence that the directive to "rejoice always" is first in that list of commands.

3. Campolo, *Kingdom of God*, 25–32.

4. See, e.g., Tuland, "Three Tithes."

5. Num 18:21–24.

6. Deut 14:22–27.

7. Deut 14:28–29.

you desire—oxen or sheep or wine or strong drink, whatever your appetite craves. And you shall eat there before the Lord your God and rejoice, you and your household."[8] In terms of the part of the command about procuring wine or strong drink or whatever you crave, the King James Version of this verse amazingly says: "And thou shalt bestow that money for whatsoever thy soul *lusteth* after . . . " (emphasis added). The Israelites were to save 10 percent of their annual income and exhaust it on what they "lusteth after," including (or perhaps especially) booze.

People don't talk about lusting after things in a spiritual or holy context. And I think it's noteworthy that God said to get wine "or other strong drink." All varieties of alcohol were welcome. And then they were to have a feast before God himself and were further commanded to "rejoice." In other words, have a huge party, and bring plenty of alcohol.

It's important at this point to acknowledge the harm that can befall not only those who struggle with alcohol abuse and addiction, but also others around them. I think it's safe to say that everybody knows of somebody who has run into trouble or caused trouble from imbibing too much, even for just one night. The biblical command is clear about not drinking too much,[9] and the Bible also has stories of bad things happening when people drink too much.[10] However, I do not want to shy away from talking about alcohol in this portion of the book. Biblical accounts are also clear about alcohol's place in contributing to the joyous celebrations that flow from faith as I describe in various parts of this book. We must thus exercise prudent judgment between amplifying a joyful

---

8. Deut 14:26.

9. See, e.g., Eph 5:18 ("And do not get drunk with wine").

10. Some examples of people who run into trouble after drinking too much include: Noah, whose sons found him lying naked (Gen 9:20–24); Lot, who is probably the worst example when he engaged in incest with his daughters not once but twice (Gen 19:30–38); King Elah of Israel, who was assassinated while drunk (1 Kgs 16:8–10); and King Ben-hadad of Syria, who "was drinking himself drunk" before Israel repelled and defeated his invading army (1 Kgs 20:1–21).

experience with alcohol and marring that joyful experience by taking things too far with the alcohol.

Returning to the command to commit 10 percent of one's income for a party every year, let me try to put into perspective what that meant for each individual and household. The median household income in the United States is currently about $67,500.[11] If that command were in effect where I live today, people earning that median income would have to spend close to $7,000 on food, booze, and whatever else they "lusteth after" for an enormous party *each year*. If somebody with a family of four earns an income at the current federal poverty level of $27,750,[12] that person would have to spend more than $2,700 each year for the party. And if you're a millionaire, you'll have to set aside $100,000 every year! That is a lot of money these people could be using for more useful things. Why would God *command* his people to spend a whole 10 percent of their hard-earned money for a single party every year? It's a huge sum for anybody to spend.

"[I]t is in partying that we know a little something about the kind of God we have."[13] Indeed, Jesus describes the kingdom of God as being like a wedding feast.[14] And of course, a proper wedding feast must have delectable food, ample alcohol, and lively music to get people on the dance floor. Yes, that's how I imagine a good wedding in present times, but indications are that weddings in biblical times were also vivacious affairs. Jesus' first miracle was at a wedding that had (*gasp*) *run out of wine*.[15] He addressed this humiliating disaster by turning enough water into wine to fill six stone jars that *each* held at least 20 gallons. That's at least 120 gallons altogether, and let's not forget that the wedding guests had already consumed all of the alcohol that was originally there, which I presume was not a small amount.

---

11. Shrider et al., "Income and Poverty," 1.
12. US Dept. of Health & Human Services, "Annual Update."
13. Campolo, *Kingdom of God*, 28.
14. Matt 22:2 ("The kingdom of heaven may be compared to a king who gave a wedding feast for his son").
15. John 2:1–11.

Jesus' first miracle was thus to prevent a party from fizzling out; he kept the party going![16] At the risk of sounding provocative or even blasphemous, I think this first miracle was Jesus' endorsement of having a good time, and he was in such a habit of breaking bread and drinking with others that some accused him of being a glutton and drunkard.[17]

And it's not surprising that the father of the prodigal son threw a raucous feast when the son came back home.[18] It is a joyous party-loving God who fills the eternity in our hearts, and that kind of joy can only burst forth from inside to be showered on others. "Salvation is joy in God which expresses itself in joy in and with one's neighbor."[19] You can't have a party with just one person, and there must be a sharing of joy among people to have a party.

Hope

Of course, not everything in life is perfect. Jesus himself wept at the loss of a loved one,[20] and there is indeed "a time to weep, and a time to laugh; a time to mourn and a time to dance."[21] There is even a whole book called "Lamentations" in the Bible to mourn the fall of Jerusalem to the Babylonians. There is no denying that we will face difficult times of loss, injustice, and general misfortune. And no matter how much we plan for good things to occur, things just don't go to plan sometimes and we experience disappointments.

---

16. Credit for this point about Jesus' first miracle goes to a guest speaker at a summer retreat when I attended Korean Baptist Church. The title of the sermon was something to the effect of, "Jesus Keeps the Party Going." Like most of the other sermons I've cited, I don't remember the name of the preacher nor when exactly I heard it.

17. Luke 7:34 (Jesus referring to himself: "The Son of Man has come eating and drinking, and you say, 'Look at him! A glutton and a drunkard, a friend of tax collectors and sinners!'"). See chapter 2, notes 28–34 above about associating with tax collectors and sinners.

18. See chapter 3, notes 58, 75–76 above.

19. Manning, *Ragamuffin Gospel*, 63

20. John 11:35 ("Jesus wept."). This is the shortest verse in the Bible.

21. Eccl 3:4.

The boxer Mike Tyson acknowledged this truth colorfully when he said: "Everybody has a plan until they get punched in the mouth."[22] Life is often painful and sad, and the natural and proper reaction during those periods is one of somberness.

However, even the book of Lamentations reminds us that there is reason for hope even in the darkest times: "The steadfast love of the Lord never ceases; his mercies never come to an end; they are new every morning; great is your faithfulness. 'The Lord is my portion,' says my soul, 'therefore I will hope in him.'"[23] And the country music artist Gary Allan acknowledges this even in the title of his song "Every Storm (Runs Out of Rain)."[24] Faith necessarily brings out hope. We need only go back to Heb 11:1 and its definition of faith: "Now faith is the assurance of things *hoped* for, the conviction of things not seen."[25] It was faith that encouraged the sick in the Bible to pursue Jesus in the hope that he would heal them. And for people who have invited God into their hearts, there is also a deeper and more timeless dimension to hope.

When somebody dies, people often say that the deceased will go to heaven. That is actually untrue; nobody goes to heaven when they die. Revelation 21 and 22 show that sometime in the future, Jesus comes to earth to remake heaven and earth, and heaven comes down to earth, where people in their resurrected bodies live.[26] In that light, we have to be careful not to misinterpret what Jesus says: "In my Father's house are many rooms. If it were not

---

22. Berardino, "Mike Tyson."
23. Lam 3:22–24.
24. Gary Allan, "Every Storm," *Set You Free* (2012).
25. Emphasis added. See also chapter 1, note 1 above.
26. Regarding the resurrection of the body, see, e.g., 1 Cor 15:51–54 ("Behold! I tell you a mystery. We shall not all sleep, but we shall all be changed, in a moment, in the twinkling of an eye, at the last trumpet. For the trumpet will sound, and the dead will be raised imperishable, and we shall be changed. For this perishable body must put on the imperishable, and this mortal body must put on immortality. When the perishable puts on the imperishable, and the mortal puts on immortality, then shall come to pass the saying that is written: 'Death is swallowed up in victory.'"). On the topic of the renewal of heaven, earth, and our bodies, see Wright, *Surprised by Hope*.

so, would I have told you that I go to prepare a place for you?"[27] Many people think that this house represents heaven—that Jesus is preparing a room for us in heaven. "But the word for '[house]' here, *monai*, is regularly used in ancient Greek not for a final resting place but for a temporary halt on a journey that will take you somewhere else in the long run."[28] After that temporary stay, we will be going to the new earth in our new bodies when it's ready.

Why am I arguing that people are wrong about leaving everything in this world and going to heaven? It's because the idea of a renewed earth will instill in us a hope that what we do today will have meaning that stretches into eternity.

The idea of being resurrected and living on a new earth is starkly different from the common understanding that in the apocalyptic last days, God will destroy the earth along with everything in it while we float to heaven to live there in eternity. Although the account in Revelation indeed illustrates cataclysmic events in the last days, that account also states that God will ultimately renew everything for the new earth. Thus, what we do today matters because it will all be reflected in the new earth where we'll live. I'll yield the floor for somebody else more capable to explain:

> The point of the resurrection, as Paul has been arguing throughout [1 Corinthians], is that *the present bodily life is not valueless because it will die*. God will raise it to new life. What you do with your body in the present matters because God has a great future in store for it. [This] certainly applies to the various vocations to which God's people are called. What you *do* in the present—by painting, preaching, singing, sewing, praying, teaching, building hospitals, digging wells, campaigning for justice, writing poems, caring for the needy, loving your neighbor as yourself—*will last into God's future*. These activities are not simply ways of making the present life a little less beastly, a little more bearable, until the day when we leave it behind altogether (as the hymn so mistakenly puts it, "Until that day when all the blest to

---

27. John 14:2.
28. Wright, *Surprised by Hope*, 150.

endless rest are called away"). They are part of what we may call *building for God's kingdom*.[29]

And we've already established that God's kingdom is a party.[30] All that we do now will be in furtherance of this divine party.

Thus, a faith that Jesus came to earth to forgive us our sins through his work on the cross necessitates the added faith that he will come again to restore us and everything else in this world.[31] In turn, we not only find meaning through God's presence in our hearts, but we also find meaning in what we *do*. Many people wonder what their legacies will be—what their impressions will be on this world. Faith in God gives us the hope that through what we do during our mortal everyday lives, we will indeed leave a mark on this planet not just for a number of years or a few generations, but in perpetuity.

Love

The Apostle Paul says that "the fruit of the Spirit is love, joy, peace, patience, kindness, goodness, faithfulness, gentleness, self-control; against such things there is no law."[32] Notice that love is listed first among all those fruits, and I don't think that's a coincidence. Love is the most important on that list. "It is thus clear that a great part of true religion consists in the affections. Love is not just one of the affections; it is the first and chief affection, the strength of the others."[33]

---

29. Wright, *Surprised by Hope*, 193 (emphases in original).

30. See notes 3–19 above.

31. I learned this point from a sermon I heard while attending a Sunday morning service on June 22, 2008, at the Mississippi Korean Baptist Church in Biloxi, Mississippi. The sermon was delivered in Korean by their senior pastor at the time, Rev. Sung Kwang Choi. The statement I most remember went something like this in my translation from Korean: "It is not enough for Christians to believe that Jesus came to save us from our sins. A complete Christian faith also believes that Jesus will come again to make this world anew."

32. Gal 5:22–23.

33. Edwards, *Religious Affections*, 15.

Where Does Faith Lead?

That's why the Bible's two greatest commandments deal with love: (1) "You shall love the Lord your God with all your heart and with all your soul and with all your mind"; and (2) "You shall love your neighbor as yourself."[34] And God himself demonstrated love to us through the work of Jesus: "For God so loved the world, that he gave his only Son, that whoever believes in him should not perish but have eternal life. For God did not send his Son into the world to condemn the world, but in order that the world might be saved through him."[35] In turn, we love others: "We love because he first loved us."[36] So the Roman poet Virgil's famous verse on love echoes what is in the Bible: "Love conquers all."[37]

But once one becomes a person of faith, the resulting outgrowth of love is to be directed especially at a particular set of people: the poor, needy, and ignored. Showing love to the poor was the law among the Israelites in the Old Testament. I've mentioned the tithe every three years that should go to the needy,[38] and there were other laws that required the people of Israel to be mindful of the poor. For example, when they harvested their land, they were prohibited from doing so all the way to the edge of their land or harvesting the land a second time. The unharvested crop had to be left for the poor and foreigner.[39] There are multiple other commands in the Old Testament to care for the needy,[40] and the

---

34. Matt 22:34–40. See also Mark 12:28–31.
35. John 3:16–17.
36. 1 John 4:19.
37. Virgil, *Eclogues*, Eclogue X, line 69 ("omnia uincit amor").
38. See note 7 above.
39. Lev 19:9–10 ("When you reap the harvest of your land, you shall not reap your field right up to its edge, neither shall you gather the gleanings after your harvest. And you shall not strip your vineyard bare, neither shall you gather the fallen grapes of your vineyard. You shall leave them for the poor and for the sojourner: I am the Lord your God.").
40. See, e.g., Lev 25:35–36; Deut 15:7–11; and Ps 82:3–4.

Bible adds that when people show kindness to the poor, it directly honors God[41] and even puts him in their debt.[42]

And Jesus continued the emphasis on loving those at the bottom of the social ladder when he spent so much of his days with not only the poor, needy, and ignored, but also with those who were absolutely despised like the prostitutes and tax collectors. It's undeniable that Jesus cared deeply about those who are considered the dregs of society. He went as far as telling the host of a dinner that when he gives a banquet, he would be blessed if he invited those who wouldn't be able to pay him back: the poor, the crippled, the lame, the blind.[43] It's interesting that Jesus uses a banquet for his illustration again. If the kingdom of God is indeed a banquet or party, we are to invite those people of humble status whom God cares about so much. The poor are so important to Jesus that he says when we feed, clothe, and care for the poor, we are actually doing it for God; and whenever we ignore the poor, we are ignoring him.[44]

Here's a story from Pastor Campolo as an illustration of what it means to invite the poor to God's party.[45] He was in Honolulu once for a speaking engagement, but because of severe jet lag he was wide awake in the middle of the night. So he went to a greasy spoon at 3:30 in the morning for a donut and coffee. While he was consuming his grub, a group of prostitutes barged in talking loud and crude. During their boisterous and dirty conversation, the woman from that group who was sitting next to him said it was going to be her birthday the next day, and another of the ladies meanly and sarcastically retorted, "So what do you want from me? A birthday party?" The woman replied meekly she was just telling people it was her birthday. She added she had never had a birthday

---

41. Prov 14:31 ("Whoever oppresses a poor man insults his Maker, but he who is generous to the needy honors him.").

42. Prov 19:17 ("Whoever is generous to the poor lends to the Lord, and he will repay him for his deed.").

43. Luke 14:12–14.

44. Matt 25:31–46.

45. This story is from Campolo, *Kingdom of God*, 3–8.

party in her life. The pastor found out that those ladies came to the diner around that time every night, so he asked the owner if he could throw a birthday party for that woman. Long story short, they had a big party for her the next evening with a big cake and decorations, and the lady was so overcome that she started crying at the end.

How would I think of myself if nobody has ever thrown a birthday party for me, if nobody thought of me as worthwhile enough to celebrate the day that I came into the world? And I wonder how many wedding banquets and other gatherings I would be invited to if I were somebody at the lowest rungs of society as a prostitute, thief, or homeless. Probably none. You just don't see people like that at many wedding banquets. But we'll see them at God's banquets—lots of them. "But anybody who reads the New Testament will discover a Jesus who loved to party with whores and with all kinds of left-out people. The publicans and 'sinners' loved him because he partied with them. The lepers of society found in him someone who would eat and drink with them. And while the solemnly pious could not relate to what he was about, those lonely people who usually didn't get invited to parties took to him with excitement."[46]

Why did they take to Jesus in excitement? Because receiving an invitation to a banquet means that they're worthwhile. The person throwing the party wants their company even though they're ignored or cast aside by everybody else. And that is what love does: it acknowledges one's worth and meaning. When we receive God's love through his presence in our hearts, it reveals a meaning in our lives when we commune with our Maker. Likewise, the ensuing love that flows from us has the power to help those whose value and contribution to the world seem so small or even absent to realize worth and meaning in themselves. An Eastern Orthodox monk on Mount Athos puts it this way:

> Parents urge their children to excel so that they may be useful to society. Based on our spiritual tradition I prefer to see human beings first and foremost in terms of who

46. Campolo, *Kingdom of God*, 9.

they are and only after that in terms of their contributions to society. Otherwise, we run the risk of turning people into machines that produce useful things. So what if you do not produce useful things? Does that mean that you should be discarded as a useless object?[47]

In that light, I think of love as picking up those who are discarded and letting them know they're worth keeping.

Showing Love through Justice

While we're talking about sharing love with others, I'd like to discuss a very important way of doing so: pursuing justice on behalf of those who are abused, downtrodden, and ignored. God repeatedly commands his believers to do this,[48] and it's even said that doing the work of justice is more acceptable to God than sacrifice.[49]

And of course, Jesus was all about delivering justice for the meek. My favorite story of his standing up for the downtrodden and abused is when Jesus defends the woman who is about to be stoned for adultery.[50] It's an astounding display of what really good criminal defense attorneys can do for the accused. The story begins with Jesus in the temple courts, and a bunch of religious

---

47. Markides, *Mountain of Silence*, 36 (quoting Father Maximos). Father Maximos continues by observing that this tendency to value ourselves based on our contributions causes "all sorts of psychological problems" that he witnesses often during confessions.

48. See, e.g., Isa 1:17 ("learn to do good; seek justice, correct oppression; bring justice to the fatherless, plead the widow's cause."); Prov 31:8–9 ("Open your mouth for the mute, for the rights of all who are destitute. Open your mouth, judge righteously, defend the rights of the poor and needy."); and Jas 1:27 ("Religion that is pure and undefiled before God the Father is this: to visit orphans and widows in their affliction, and to keep oneself unstained from the world.").

49. Prov 21:3 ("To do righteousness and justice is more acceptable to the Lord than sacrifice."). See also Matt 23:23 ("Woe to you, scribes and Pharisees, hypocrites! For you tithe mint and dill and cumin, and have neglected the weightier matters of the law: justice and mercy and faithfulness. These you ought to have done, without neglecting the others.").

50. John 7:53—8:11.

leaders bring before him a woman who has been caught in the act of adultery. They tell Jesus the situation, remind him that the Law of Moses commands the stoning of an adulteress, and inquire what should be done. (This penalty of death for adultery was permitted by the Roman government that ruled Israel at the time.)[51]

The question is a trap. If Jesus responds that the woman should be shown mercy, the religious leaders will accuse him of not honoring the sacred Law of Moses and condoning the heinous sin of adultery. But if Jesus instructs the learned men to stone her, they would accuse him of contradicting everything he had been teaching by being so heartless and unmerciful.

Maybe the woman was set up by the religious leaders for this showdown with Jesus. When people sleep with somebody they shouldn't sleep with, they generally try to keep it secret. However, it is recorded that she was caught in the act. Those religious leaders must have known that the woman was up to no good with another man, and I'm thinking they concealed themselves somewhere within sight of where the hanky-panky was going to happen. How else would they catch her in the act?

I have further basis for believing this was a setup as well: where's the man she slept with? Why catch and bring only the woman? The applicable Law of Moses applies to both the adulterer and the adulteress: "If a man is found lying with the wife of another man, *both of them shall die, the man who lay with the woman, and the woman.* So you shall purge the evil from Israel."[52] If the religious leaders are truly concerned about "justice," they would have brought both the man and woman. (But maybe the man was part of the setup too?)

Anyway, it's just the woman standing accused in this story, and Jesus raises perhaps the greatest defense in history for a criminal trial that holds capital punishment in the balance. He challenges any of the accusers who is without sin to carry out the execution: "Let him who is without sin among you be the first to

---

51. Henry, *Commentary on the Whole Bible*, 1964.

52. Deut 22:22 (emphasis added). See also chapter 3, note 45 above (citing this law in the story of David and Bathsheba).

throw a stone at her."⁵³ Of course, nobody is sinless, so the accusers leave the scene, and the woman is acquitted.

There was never any dispute in the facts of this case: the woman slept with a man she shouldn't have slept with, and there is no record of her denying it. And there was never any dispute regarding which law applies. I apologize for speaking like an attorney, but the issue that Jesus raised was procedural, not substantive. Who has the authority to prosecute and judge another? (Or in legal parlance, who has jurisdiction over this matter?) It's one thing if the religious leaders sought insight from Jesus on what to do for justice to be properly served, but it's another thing entirely to use justice as a prop for discrediting Jesus. They were so unmoored from morality that they were willing to have a woman be stoned to death so that they could corner Jesus. The hearts of these religious leaders were not truly in pursuit of justice as God has commanded,⁵⁴ and Jesus' defense on behalf of the woman was that they were thus lacking in authority and jurisdiction even to partake in this matter.

Justice is thus not just a matter of figuring out whether or not one has sinned.⁵⁵ This is clear from how much Jesus shared life with people who were undoubtedly sinners, including tax collectors and prostitutes. Rather, justice for those who have Jesus residing in their hearts is to show the same mercy that God has shown them. I've stated in chapter 2 that an important and necessary element of attaining the faith that brings God to one's heart is to acknowledge the absolute corrupt state of our being. It is because of

---

53. John 8:7.

54. See note 48 above.

55. I'm fully aware, especially in my capacity as a practicing attorney, that the administration of justice must involve ascertaining whether there is wrongdoing. I also won't deny that justice requires carrying out consequences in proportion to the severity of the wrongdoing and its effects. Those consequences should achieve the ends of deterrence, restoration, and punishment through such means as financial restitution, prison terms, and other measures of equity. But please notice that I say justice is "*not just* a matter of figuring out whether or not one has sinned." As I explain further below, justice also involves the exercise of love.

the work of Jesus on the cross to take the punishment of sin in our place that we can even think of God fulfilling our hearts. A proper perspective on justice for those in the faith involves the desire for others to experience the same awesome mercy that we've received. "Be merciful, even as your Father is merciful. Judge not, and you will not be judged; condemn not, and you will not be condemned; forgive, and you will be forgiven."[56]

Pursuing Justice in Our Day-to-Day Lives

Justice doesn't necessarily require dramatic acts like defending someone in a death penalty trial. At its core, loving others through justice is merely including those who are on the outside and overlooked. The legendary sportswriter Shirley Povich of *The Washington Post* was a proponent of desegregating professional sports as far back as the 1930s,[57] but his desire to set things right in society led him to practice this inclusivity in his day-to-day work.

A beautiful example of his low-key approach to justice occurred in 1942 when Mr. Povich was at Griffith Stadium in Washington, DC, to cover a boxing match.[58] He was in the press box preparing for the fight to begin when he saw another sportswriter who would also go on to become legendary in his own right, Sam Lacy of *The Baltimore Afro-American*. Mr. Povich asked him why he was standing around, and Mr. Lacy replied that he had a press pass but no seat. A black man like Mr. Lacy wasn't welcome among the group of white sportswriters in the press box. Mr. Povich then invited Mr. Lacy down to where he was and to take an empty seat next to him. When Mr. Lacy sat in the press box, nobody could say anything because it was Mr. Provich who invited him, and Mr. Povich had already established himself as a man above reproach. Mr. Lacy later claimed that was the beginning of seat integration in the

---

56. Luke 6:36–37.

57. Povich, *All Those Mornings*, 72. Mr. Povich was indeed ahead of his time. For example, Major League Baseball remained segregated until Jackie Robinson started a game for the Brooklyn Dodgers on April 15, 1947.

58. Povich, *All Those Mornings*, 72.

press box for sporting events, and it started with one man's simple invitation for another man to grab a seat next to him: "When somebody like Shirley would support you, all of them started to accept you."[59]

A major byproduct of faith leading to the loving pursuit of justice is bringing those who are not accepted or are on the margins of society into human company. It is saying "this person's with me" when we invite somebody unpopular to a gathering of friends, bring a "sinner" to church, or treat a homeless person to lunch. By doing so, we bring to God precisely those people whom he wants to invite to the party that is the kingdom of God. Just as it would not have come naturally for the centurion to profess that Jesus could merely say the word for his servant to be healed, acts of kindness to the unlovable certainly don't come naturally to us. But through such extraordinary acts of love for those whom others ignore, we demonstrate this faith that astonishes God.

I'll finish with this pointed observation from the Epistle of James: "What good is it, my brothers, if someone says he has faith but does not have works? Can that faith save him? If a brother or sister is poorly clothed and lacking in daily food, and one of you says to them, 'Go in peace, be warmed and filled,' without giving them the things needed for the body, what good is that? So also faith by itself, if it does not have works, is dead."[60] And a dead faith is nothing to marvel at.

---

59. Povich, *All Those Mornings*, 72.
60. Jas 2:14–17.

Conclusion

I'VE SHARED THAT DEMONSTRATIONS of faith can somehow surprise and astonish an omniscient God like how the centurion's faith amazed Jesus. To see what faith is, I looked to Heb 11:1, which describes faith as establishing a foundation so that we're sure of what we hope for and serving as proof of those things that are unseen. Namely, faith sets things up so that God can fulfill the eternal longing for worth and meaning in our hearts. Attaining this kind of faith isn't easy, but God will work with us even if we can muster only a small amount of faith—even faith as small as a mustard seed or 1/4 of a cent. However, we need to give it all we have to muster even that tiny bit of faith.

We also need to acknowledge that our corrupted state doesn't naturally allow us to reach the requisite amount of faith. We further need to believe that Jesus allows us to commune with God because he paid the ultimate price of death for our natural corruption and then overcame it with his resurrection. Once we achieve faith so that God resides in us, it can be difficult to maintain faith because of our natural undulations, but we need to keep at it. Finally, when we obtain and maintain the faith that allows our hearts to be satisfied by God, we will naturally share the joy, hope, and love that wells up from our hearts. This includes pursuing justice for those who are on the fringes or are outside of general society.

Obtaining and maintaining faith in God is really hard; it's inhuman. But thankfully, faith isn't ultimately the result of anything we do. It is the grace of God embracing us even when we're as bad as the prodigal son, or worse. "All the persons of faith I know are sinners, doubters, uneven performers. We are secure not because we are sure of ourselves but because we trust that God is sure of us."[1] And this is how we exhibit faith that leads God to marvel.

We might be tempted to think that once we have obtained and maintained faith, we need to do amazing and miraculous things like the apostles in the New Testament or famous bearers of the faith like Rev. Martin Luther King Jr. or Mother Teresa. However, God simply wants us to shine his light, and he doesn't say it has to be done in an extraordinary way.[2]

When Jesus was taken aback by the centurion's faith, the centurion wasn't doing anything on the level of changing the course of human history. He was simply demonstrating love and concern for his servant, and he exercised his faith in Jesus by asking him to cure the servant. How many hurting people do we know around us who would appreciate a friend simply asking God on their behalf to intervene?

And look at the book of Acts as another example. The book is filled with stories of the apostles traveling to distant places, working miracles, and bringing thousands of people to God at a time. But the book ends anticlimactically in its final verses with a rather humdrum scene of how the Apostle Paul spent his days under house arrest in Rome: "He lived there two whole years at his own expense, and welcomed all who came to him, proclaiming the kingdom of God and teaching about the Lord Jesus Christ with all boldness and without hindrance."[3] The Apostle Paul just hung out in the home he rented, and he shared about God while accepting

---

1. Peterson, *Long Obedience*, 90.

2. See Matt 5:16 ("let your light shine before others, so that they may see your good works and give glory to your Father who is in heaven.").

3. Acts 28:30–31 (The King James Version and New International Version say more plainly that Paul rented the house). How Paul ended up under house arrest in Rome is a long story, but the gist is that the Romans arrested him during a riot that started after he was falsely accused of defiling the temple in Jerusalem. Paul then appealed to Caesar as a Roman citizen, which led the authorities to transfer him to the courts in Rome. The account of Paul's ordeal starts in Acts 21.

Conclusion

guests.[4] That is perhaps the extent to how most of us will live out our faith: most likely not under house arrest, but taking advantage of little opportunities to share about our faith while spending time with people. It's not much, but there is no shame in that.[5] Marvelous faith is marvelous faith, no matter how extraordinary or dull the circumstances are in our lives.

---

[4]. Many believe that Paul's house arrest actually allowed him to evangelize more effectively. Anybody interested in his teaching could visit him, and the religious authorities who objected to his teaching could not lay a hand on him while under Roman custody. Henry, *Commentary on the Whole Bible*, 2192. Also, "his friends were allowed free access to him, and in this way there was probably a wider and more effectual opening for his personal influence than if he had spoken publicly, and so exposed himself to the risk of an organised antagonism." Ellicott, *Commentary on the Whole Bible*, 184.

[5]. Credit for this observation about the final scene in Acts goes to a preacher I heard during a Sunday morning service at the Christ Church Cathedral in Oxford, England, during the summer of 2007.

Bibliography

à Kempis, Thomas. *Imitation of Christ*. Nashville: Thomas Nelson, 1999.
Arias, Elizabeth, and Jiaquan Xu. "United States Life Tables, 2018." *National Vital Statistics Reports* 69.12 (Nov. 17, 2020) 1–45. https://www.cdc.gov/nchs/data/nvsr/nvsr69/nvsr69-12-508.pdf.
Bailey, Kenneth E. *The Cross and the Prodigal: Luke 15 through the Eyes of Middle Eastern Peasants*. 2nd ed. Downers Grove, IL: InterVarsity, 2005.
Bennett, Chris. "Grizzly Hell: USDA Worker Survives Epic Bear Attack." *Farm Journal*, January 4, 2021. https://www.agweb.com/news/crops/crop-production/grizzly-hell-usda-worker-survives-epic-bear-attack.
Berardino, Mike. "Mike Tyson Explains One of His Most Famous Quotes." *South Florida Sun Sentinel*, November 9, 2012. https://www.sun-sentinel.com/sports/fl-xpm-2012-11-09-sfl-mike-tyson-explains-one-of-his-most-famous-quotes-20121109-story.html.
Blow, Charles M. "Religious Constriction." *New York Times*, June 8, 2014. https://www.nytimes.com/2014/06/09/opinion/blow-religious-constriction.html.
Boice, James Montgomery. *Psalms*. Vol. 1. Grand Rapids, MI: Baker, 2005.
Boyd, Gregory A., and Edward K. Boyd. *Letters from a Skeptic: A Son Wrestles with His Father's Questions about Christianity*. 2nd ed. Colorado Springs: David C. Cook, 2008.
Campolo, Tony. *Carpe Diem: Seize the Day*. Nashville: W Publishing Group, 1994.
———. *The Kingdom of God Is a Party: God's Radical Plan for His Family*. Dallas: Word, 1990.
Curtis, Ken. "Whatever Happened to the Twelve Disciples?" Christianity.com, April 28, 2010. https://www.christianity.com/church/church-history/timeline/1-300/whatever-happened-to-the-twelve-apostles-11629558.html.
de Becker, Gavin. *The Gift of Fear: Survival Signs That Protect Us from Violence*. New York: Back Bay, 2021.
Edwards, Jonathan. *Religious Affections: A Christian's Character Before God*. Vancouver, BC: Regent College Publishing, 2003.

Bibliography

Ellicott, Charles J. *Commentary on the Whole Bible*. Vol. VII. Eugene, OR: Wipf & Stock, 2015.

ESV Study Bible. Personal Size. Wheaton, IL: Crossway, 2008.

Fahmy, Dalia. "Key Findings about Americans' Belief in God." Pew Research Center, April 25, 2018. https://www.pewresearch.org/fact-tank/2018/04/25/key-findings-about-americans-belief-in-god/.

Friedrichsen, Timothy A. "The Temple, a Pharisee, a Tax Collector, and the Kingdom of God: Rereading a Jesus Parable (Luke 18:10–14A)." *Journal of Biblical Literature* 124.1 (Spring 2005) 89–119.

Guzik, David. "2 Samuel 12—Nathan Confronts David." Enduring Word, n.d. https://enduringword.com/bible-commentary/2-samuel-12/.

Henry, Matthew. *Commentary on the Whole Bible: Complete and Unabridged*. 14th printing. Peabody, MA: Hendrickson, 2003.

International Commission on English in the Liturgy Corporation. *The Roman Missal: English Translation According to the Third Typical Edition*. Washington, DC: United States Conference of Catholic Bishops, 2011.

John Paul II. *Crossing the Threshold of Hope*. New York: Alfred A. Knopf, 1994.

Kaneda, Toshiko, and Carl Haub. "How Many People Have Ever Lived on Earth?" Population Reference Bureau (May 18, 2021). https://www.prb.org/articles/how-many-people-have-ever-lived-on-earth/.

Lewis, C. S. *Mere Christianity*. New York: HarperSanFrancisco, 2001.

———. *The Screwtape Letters*. New York: HarperSanFrancisco, 2001.

Life Application Study Bible (New International Version). 3rd ed. Carol Stream, IL: Tyndale, 2019.

Lyall, Francis. *Slaves, Citizens, Sons: Legal Metaphors in the Epistles*. Grand Rapids, MI: Academie, 1984.

MacArthur, John. *The Prodigal Son: An Astonishing Study of the Parable Jesus Told to Unveil God's Grace for You*. Nashville: Thomas Nelson, 2008.

Macfarlane, Roger T. "Hebrew, Aramaic, Greek, and Latin: Languages of New Testament Judea." *Brigham Young University Studies* 36.3 (1996–97) 228–38.

Manning, Brennan. *The Ragamuffin Gospel*. Sisters, OR: Multnomah, 2000.

Markides, Kyriacos C. *The Mountain of Silence: A Search for Orthodox Spirituality*. New York: Image, 2001.

Martin, James, SJ. *Between Heaven and Mirth: Why Joy, Humor, and Laughter Are at the Heart of the Spiritual Life*. New York: HarperOne, 2011.

McCarthy, Pádraig. "The Challenge of Translation." *The Furrow* 62.3 (March 2011) 131–38.

Merriam-Webster. "Awe." www.merriam-webster.com/dictionary/awe.

———. "Awesome." www.merriam-webster.com/dictionary/awesome.

———. "Conviction." www.merriam-webster.com/dictionary/conviction.

———. "Pharisee." www.merriam-webster.com/dictionary/pharisee.

Moore, Steven Dean, dir. "The Joy of Sect." *The Simpsons*, season 9, episode 13. Aired February 8, 1998 on the Fox network.

Bibliography

The Notorious B.I.G. *Life After Death*. Bad Boy Records 78612-73011-2, 1997, compact disc.

Peterson, Eugene H. *A Long Obedience in the Same Direction: Discipleship in an Instant Society*. 2nd ed. Downers Grove, IL: InterVarsity, 2000.

———. *The Message: The Bible in Contemporary Language*. Colorado Springs: NavPress, 2014.

Piper, John. *A Hunger for God: Desiring God through Fasting and Prayer*. Wheaton, IL: Crossway, 2013.

Povich, Shirley. *All Those Mornings . . . At the Post*. Edited by Lynn Povich et al. New York: Public Affairs, 2005.

Puskas, Charles B., and C. Michael Robbins. *An Introduction to the New Testament*. 2nd ed. Eugene, OR: Cascade, 2011.

Shrider, Emily A., et al. "Income and Poverty in the United States: 2020." U.S. Census Bureau (Issued September 2021).

Spencer, Reid. "Joey Logano Still Identified with 2009 at Dover." NASCAR, May 4, 2018, https://www.nascar.com/news-media/2018/05/04/joey-logano-still-identified-2009-wreck-dover/.

Stein, Robert H. *The New American Commentary: An Exegetical and Theological Exposition of Holy Scripture*. Vol. 24. Nashville: B&H, 1992.

Strobel, Lee. *The Case for Christ: A Journalist's Personal Investigation of the Evidence for Jesus*. Grand Rapids, MI: Zondervan, 1998.

Strong, James. *The New Exhaustive Concordance of the Bible*. Nashville: Thomas Nelson, 1996.

Taylor, Jennifer. "The Widow's Mite." Samford University Special Collection Treasures (July 2005). https://library.samford.edu/special/treasures/2005/mite.html.

Thompson, James W. *Hebrews*. Paideia Commentaries on the New Testament. Grand Rapids, MI: Baker Academic, 2008.

Tugwell, Simon. *The Beatitudes: Soundings in Christian Traditions*. Springfield, IL: Templegate, 1980.

Tuland, C. G. "The Three Tithes of the Old Testament." *Ministry International Journal for Pastors* (September 1958). https://www.ministrymagazine.org/archive/1958/09/the-three-tithes-of-the-old-testament.

Turner, Paul. *Understanding the Revised Mass Texts*. Leader's Edition, 2nd ed. Chicago: Liturgy Training, 2010.

Twain, Mark. *Following the Equator: A Journey around the World*. Scotts Valley, CA: CreateSpace, 2017.

US Dept. of Health & Human Services. "Annual Update of the HHS Poverty Guidelines." Federal Register 87.14 (Jan. 21, 2022) 3315–16. https://www.federalregister.gov/documents/2022/01/21/2022-01166/annual-update-of-the-hhs-poverty-guidelines.

Virgil. *The Eclogues*. Translated by Guy Lee. New York: Penguin, 1984.

Wikipedia. "Greek Lepton." Last modified February 21, 2021. https://en.wikipedia.org/wiki/Greek_lepton.

Bibliography

———. "Mustard Seed." Last modified July 12, 2021. https://en.wikipedia.org/wiki/Mustard_seed.

Wright, N. T. *Surprised by Hope: Rethinking Heaven, the Resurrection, and the Mission of the Church*. New York: HarperOne, 2008.

www.ingramcontent.com/pod-product-compliance
Lightning Source LLC
Chambersburg PA
CBHW071159090426
42736CB00012B/2385